THE

OSIRIS
TESTAMENT

Genesis of the Phoenix

STEPHEN H. PROVOST

To my mother, who showed me how to rise from the ashes.

Praise for other works by the author

"The complex idea of mixing morality and mortality is a fresh twist on the human condition. ... **Memortality** is one of those books that will incite more questions than it answers. And for fandom, that's a good thing."

— Ricky L. Brown, Amazing Stories

"Punchy and fast paced, **Memortality** reads like a graphic novel. ... (Provost's) style makes the trippy landscapes and mind-bending plot points more believable and adds a thrilling edge to this vivid crossover fantasy."

— Foreword Reviews

"Whether a troubled family's curse or the nightmarish hell created by a new kind of A.I., the autopsy of a vampire or Santa's darker side ... Provost's sure hand guides you down gloomy avenues you do not expect."

— Mark Onspaugh, author of The Faceless One
and Deadlight Jack, on **Nightmare's Eve**

"**Memortality** by Stephen Provost is a highly original, thrilling novel unlike anything else out there."

— David McAfee, bestselling author of
33 A.D., 61 A.D., and 79 A.D.

"Profusely illustrated throughout, **Highway 99** is unreservedly recommended as an essential and core addition to every community and academic library's California History collections."

— California Bookwatch

"As informed and informative as it is entertaining and absorbing, **Fresno Growing Up** is very highly recommended for personal, community, and academic library 20th Century American History collections."

— John Burroughs, Reviewer's Bookwatch

Contents

Preface

Majestic. Brutal. Inspired. Judgmental. Groundbreaking. Hypocritical. These just a few of the terms I've heard used to describe the Hebrew scriptures, known to Christians as the "Old Testament." This body of literature, written by a wide variety of individuals over a period of several hundred years, represents (as one would suspect) a wide variety of perspectives and purposes.

One thing most of it shares in common, however, is its nationalism. Most of the authors and, more importantly, those who assembled their works in a single collection, wanted to create a narrative for the Judean/Israelite people. It was meant, in simplest terms, as a national narrative. It wasn't intended to be read or appreciated by non-Israelis; it was written to promote a national agenda and, more specifically, the agenda of those in power at the time it was compiled.

The Old Testament hardly alone in this. In fact, most nations, if they're around for any length of time, develop their own narratives — which identify them as special or chosen.

Ideally, they'll focus on the positives. This is, after all, an exercise in positive spin. But every nation makes mistakes, and some of them are whoppers. The Soviet Union dealt with these mistakes by trying to cover them up, rewriting history as though they never even happened … which can be awkward when the mistakes are already so well known that denying them would compromise the storyteller's credibility. Of course, a nation can always use force (or the threat of it) to silence those who dare to contradict the official narrative, and many nations have done so.

Over a period of centuries, however, such pressure is hard to maintain. Regimes will come and go, and some will certainly be more tolerant of alternative views than others. Some will also be weaker than others and less able to enforce adherence to the "party line." In such cases, denying historical events becomes more difficult, and narrators may be forced to fall back on Plan B: rationalization. If you can't deny that something occurred, "spin" it so it still supports your case.

Doubtless the Hebrew scribes and editors would have loved to present their own nation as one that never lost any wars, its leaders as men who never engaged in any immoral acts, its heroes as people who never made mistakes. But this just wasn't possible for a nation repeatedly torn apart by internal strife and intrigue, while also being continually assailed by stronger nations that succeeded in dominating it.

Enter the God Factor. When deity is added to the mix, it serves a couple of functions. The nationalist deity is an ideal — a model for what the nation would be like if it hadn't suffered all those embarrassing setbacks at the hands of invaders, usurpers, false prophets and the like. This allows the nation to save face in the midst of its own failings. "Those foreign invaders didn't conquer us because they're better than we are, they succeeded because we weren't living up to our own ideals. We may have failed, but our ideal — our god — did not." Judah/Israel was still inherently superior to the nations that surrounded it; the problem was its own failure to embody the ideal it was called to fulfill.

Its god (or ideal self), by the same token, was still head and shoulders above all other national gods. Never mind that the supposedly invincible "lord of hosts" repeatedly failed to lead his armies to victory against more powerful foes who worshipped different gods. This was no reflection on the ideal, but rather on the mundane nation that was failing to live up to that ideal.

This was Israel's response to its own state of cognitive dissonance, its explanation why the expectation didn't square with the reality. In order to reconcile the two, the mundane nation had to believe it was doing something wrong in the eyes of its ideal self — its god.

The presence of deity explains the failure of the people to live up to its self-designation as somehow special or superior to the nations around it. The wider the gap between the ideal and the reality, the more tenaciously a nation clung to the former in a desperate attempt to save face and preserve its elevated sense of self. In other words, to salvage its ego.

The god, in a sense, served as a sort of reverse scapegoat: a blameless entity that enables a nation to maintain its inflated sense of self. Its association with the ideal creates a sort of ethical bubble in which it can do pretty much anything it wants, yet maintain its status as "special" or "chosen."

In the final analysis, this enables a nation to have its cake and eat it, too. On the one hand, its failures are explained by its own failure to live up to its ideal self, represented by its patron god — explaining why other, supposedly inferior, nations have been able to prevail against a "chosen" race. Yet on the other hand, these failures in no way diminish the nation's specialness. Its chosen status rests not on any superior action, either in terms of ethics or military might, but rather on its core national identity. It's ultimately judged as superior not based on what it does, but on who it is.

The genius of Christianity and Islam was to expand this model beyond a strictly nationalist setting. By offering open membership, the leaders of these movements created de facto nations without borders whose potential for expansion was limited only by the number of people on the planet. People were no longer "chosen" or "special" based on their place of birth, but on their acceptance of a few simple articles of faith.

Whereas Yahweh had been the projected ideal for the nation of Israel, perfect in every sense, Jesus took on the same status within Christianity. The only change was that the scapegoating became overt: the perfect god-man was punished for the offenses of others, so that they could walk off scot free. This was the doctrine propagated by Paul of Tarsus, whose teachings became the basis for the dominant form of Christianity … none of which can be found in the words attributed to Jesus, the movement's putative founder. But while Paul's ideas weren't consistent with Jesus', the were entirely within the tradition contained in the Hebrew scriptures.

Here's how it worked. In the Old Testament, the failures of Judah/Israel to live up to the ideal of Yahweh were blamed for their failure to prevail over their enemies. But the people maintained their special status despite those failings because of their association with Yahweh. Paul (who in his writings describes himself as a fervent Jew who strove mightily to keep the law) applied the same theological model to Jesus. According to his teachings, Christians would always fail to live up to the ideal represented by Jesus because of "original sin." However, as in Judaism, they would maintain their special status —

which Paul referred to as salvation — despite those failings, because of their association with Jesus.

The model, in both cases, shares these common points.

1) Projection of an ideal self onto a god figure.
2) Placement of blame on the self for failures, which cannot be attributed to either the god figure or the actions of enemies.
3) Preservation of special status despite guilt.

In light of this, it's no wonder that the Christian canon incorporated the Hebrew scriptures, despite the jarring disconnect that many have noticed between the warlike god they present and many of the teachings attributed to Jesus. While those teachings often mark a point of significant departure from the Hebrew scriptures, the teachings of Paul offer almost seamless continuity. The difference between Paul and the Old Testament lies not in content but in the target audience: for the Old Testament writers, it was a single nation; for Paul, it was the world.

The ancient Jewish state was forged in an atmosphere of nearly continual conflict, so it's no surprise that a war/storm god rose to the head of the Jewish pantheon (the Semitic peoples were originally polytheistic in their beliefs). The title "lord of hosts" indicates that one of his prime functions was to go forth at the head of the national hosts, or armies, into battle.

This primacy of a war/storm god was hardly unique the ancient world. In Phoenicia, the storm god Baal was at the head of the pantheon. The Norse myths extolled not one but two war gods, Odin and Thor, as their most popular patrons. In Celtic myth, The Dagda was a fierce warrior. War was a fact of life, as much as the harvest, the tides and the heat of the sun were. But unlike these latter phenomena, men could gain acclaim and renown for their deeds in battle; more than this, they could gain political power. Those who began as successful field generals could claim the throne by force of arms and, when they had done so, would naturally maintain — and impose — the worship of the god they credited for their success: the war god.

Anyone who doubts of the continuity between ancient cultures and Christianity in this regard needs look no further than the event many consider decisive in the ascendance of the Christian religion. This was the battle of the Milvian Bridge between Constantine and his rival for the throne of imperial Rome, Maxentius. According to a famous story of that battle, Constantine is said to have seen the sign of the cross above the sun, accompanied by the words "in hoc signo vinces" (in this sign, conquer). Maxentius drowned in the Tiber River during the battle, and Constantine's forces prevailed. This was seen as a sign that the Christian god had endorsed him personally by acting as the lord of hosts, going before him and guaranteeing the victory.

The idea that a Jewish sage who taught his followers to turn the other cheek should have acted supernaturally by killing an emperor's rival and delivering him victory seems peculiar to the point of being comical. But once again, the person of Jesus has nothing to do with this story, which is based instead upon ancient beliefs concerning the war/storm god.

I have suggested in "The Gospel of the Phoenix" and elsewhere that Jesus himself had little to do with this god and instead associated himself with Osiris, the "father in heaven" of Egyptian lore who was associated with kingship but more closely linked to wisdom and the harvest than to warfare.

Because kings made their name and cemented their reputations by winning battles, and kings (or their scribes) most often wrote history, the scriptures and legends of ancient peoples consist largely of accounts involving war and battle. The victory steles erected by pharaohs such as Thutmose III to commemorate their victories testify to this. So do the Hebrew scriptures, which contain celebrations of carnage, pillage and conquest that would do any Viking proud.

History is, as they say, written by the winners. And the winners like to make themselves look good. Hence, a man named David — who revolted against his king, slept with a loyal soldier's wife (then had him killed in the most cowardly fashion), stood by while his daughter was raped and reneged on a promise to his best friend — is regarded in the Hebrew scriptures as the best of kings. His moral failings weren't important; what mattered was his association with Yahweh and his success on the battlefield.

In "The Gospel of the Phoenix," I set out to write a story of Jesus' life from a perspective untainted by the theology of Paul. This present work is a similar endeavor: My goal is to produce a work that offers an account of ancient myth and history not written from the perspective of a war god. The idea here is to present a text not designed to buttress the reputation of a nation, king or priesthood, but instead to provide a broader perspective. As "The Gospel of the Phoenix" included material both from the Christian canon and extracanonical sources, so "The Osiris Testament" incorporates material from a variety of traditions beyond the Hebrew texts of the Old Testament written from the narrow perspective of late monotheistic Judaism.

One challenge in writing such a book lies in the fact that, as mentioned, much ancient literature deals with battles, wars and conquests. That said, however, part of the difficulty in dealing with such literature lies the fact that it glorifies such actions — along with the often indefensible actions of the winners. The scribes often laud the actions of people who would be condemned as thugs, despots and worse today, some of whom would be open to prosecution for war crimes. What if the same actions were presented as an object lesson concerning the cruelty of armed conflict and the hypocrisy of "great" kings who were, in fact, tyrants and warmongers?

What if the gods themselves were so disgusted by the human addiction to conflict that they simply turned their backs in revulsion?

And what if, instead of adopting the inherently biased narrative of a single nation (Judah-Israel) as though it were the history of the entire world, we were to create a new narrative with a broader scope and more universal themes? This is what I have attempted here.

Another challenge in undertaking such a project is the overlap of legendary and historical accounts. Many modern writers have attempted to write "definitive" histories of ancient people or cultures. The problem is, the scribes who produced the ancient works didn't recognize a clear-cut distinction between legend and history. The editors of the Hebrew scripture recorded legends that were old, even in their own time, alongside records of recent events. People who consider these texts divinely inspired take them all literally, as though they were historically accurate (even where they contradict themselves). Historians, on the other hand, try to sift through them and separate the history from the hype.

This work isn't meant to do either. Its purpose is to provide a new perspective on myth and history, and it includes a little of both, just as the Hebrew authors and editors did. The intention here isn't to present an fully accurate history of the period covered, but instead to craft a new, broader narrative based on ancient traditions.

Many people don't realize that this is exactly what the Hebrew scribes did. They incorporated many older stories, from Mesopotamian , Egyptian and Canaanite lore, combining them into a new tradition that they could call their own. One thing I've tried to do here is separate some of those traditions from their transplanted context within the Hebrew scriptures and present them here in a their earlier form. The flood story, for instance, is related in something closer to its original form, as a story of a Sumerian king caught up in a regional crisis.

Other ancient tales have been reimagined in light of evidence not at hand or suppressed when they were first told. Still others have been woven together from several strands of tradition into entirely new stories.

The work is separated into five books, constituting a sort of alternative Pentateuch, with the first book covering a legendary period similar to the time covered in the first few chapters of Genesis; the second focusing on the first great civilization in Babylon; the third dealing with the golden age of Egypt; the fourth focusing on the Phoenician, Irish and Scandinavian cultures; and the fifth an alternative view of the events covered in the biblical Book of Samuel.

The Osiris Testament: Genesis of the Phoenix is a new tradition that encompasses much ancient lore. It's written in the same scriptural style employed in The Gospel of the Phoenix and The Way of the Phoenix, which roughly corresponded to the gospels and Hebrew wisdom literature, respectively, and completes the trilogy begun and continued in those two previous works.

I hope the reader will find it engaging, challenging and refreshing — and enjoyable.

The Book of

Eden

1

¹ In the time before times, when the world was young, the gods came together and fashioned for themselves a dwelling among the clouds to the north in the highlands.

² This place they named Aratta, which is called Ararat, and they adorned it with all manner of bounty from their storehouse, with gold and silver, and lapis lazuli. ³ It was the

land where the sky and the earth came together, for which reason they called it the Kingdom of Heaven.

[4] They named it in the ancient tongue "Anu," which means the vault of the sky, that place where the lady of the mountain dwelt. [5] It is she whose womb brings forth new life, who joins the sky above with the earth beneath and binds them together that they might bear fruit. [6] Her caves are bedecked with jewels and crystals, and gold may be found in the depths of her dwelling. [7] The clouds are her crown, and the stars are the jewels set within it.

[8] In those days there came forth from heaven the brothers Enlil and Enki, who contended fiercely with one another. [9] Enlil was given dominion over the airy heights of Aratta, and his companion was the eagle who soars across the firmament.

[10] But Enki was given the plain below called Eden, and his sigil was the serpent that was entwined about his staff.

[11] He who has ears to hear, let him hear.

The Gardener and the Vineyard

[12] It came to pass that Enki became the father to a son, Asar. He it was who became the first to harvest grain and plants, for which reason he was called "the Gardener."

[13] His beloved was Inanna, who was crowned the queen of heaven and enthroned in Aratta's heights.

[14] At her bidding did Asar plant a garden on the plain of Eden, where the soil was rich and fertile. [15] Sheltered by the

snow-covered peaks of Aratta and nourished by the waters of heaven's chalice, it was a haven for all who came to dwell there.

[16] Give heed to the words that are written here, that you may understand these secrets. For Asar is the name of Osiris, and Inanna is called also Aset, whose name is Isis.

[17] A brother and sister were born alongside them, whose names are Seth and Nephthys.

[18] In his garden, Osiris planted an orchard of trees rising up from the earth, which were pleasing to the eye and good for food. [19] In the midst of the garden he set a watchtower and a vineyard, also with its winepress.

[20] The first of these he called "the tree of life," for by ascending one could survey the open firmament and look out upon the land unto the horizon, as if from heaven itself. [21] Inanna gave it her blessing, and in her honor did he build it. Therein would she dwell.

[22] And in its heights did he set all the great lights of the firmament, like jewels for her adornment, and appointed them to keep watch over times and seasons. For this reason were they called the Watchers.

[23] The vineyard he called the "tree of knowledge, good and ill," for the fruit of the vine brought both inspiration and folly to those who might partake of it.

[24] And around about the vineyard were arrayed all manner of fern and vine, shrub and grassland, tree and orchard. [25] These were watered by a spring that went forth out of Eden and became a torrent of four great rivers.

[26] The first is the Pishon, which winds across the sands of the desert in a nation rich in gold. In this place, resin is found in plenty, and onyx is also there. [27] The second river's name is Gihon, which traverses the land of Cush. [28] The third is the Tigris, which runs before Assyria, and the fourth is the great Euphrates.

[29] Now men and women were in the midst of the garden, as newborn children at a mother's breast. The queen of heaven was a mother to them, and Osiris was their father. [30] And they were naked, clad only in the shelter of the sky.

[31] The men were called sons of Adam, which in Hebrew means "the earth" but in Egypt is rendered as Atum, who is honored in the city of the sun as creator of all men. [32] The women were called daughters of Eve, which means "giver of life," their name for holy Inanna.

[33] For this reason was Inanna herself called the "tree of life" and "the tower," which in Hebrew is rendered as Migdol or Magdala. For through her alone does man ascend unto the heavens.

[34] And the lady of the tower came to be called the Magdalene.

[35] He who has ears to hear, let him hear.

2

[1] Osiris taught the sons of Adam the way of reaping and sowing, and the means by which they might water the fields. [2] The cultivation of the grapevine did he teach them,

and the ways of wheat and barley. "For behold," he said, "It is I who created the barley and wheat to make the gods live and, after the gods, the herd of man."

³ He therefore gave them charge of all the animals that were in that place, to care for them, and he taught them the use of speech so that they might name them. ⁴ And he gave them laws, engraved in stone from the heights of Aratta, his own commandments, ten in number, that in keeping them they might prosper. These were the laws that he gave them:

⁵ Speak not in the name of any god, for such is unfettered arrogance, but let thy words redeem themselves.

⁶ Honor thy mother, who is the earth, and nourish thy children, who are fruit upon the tree of life.

⁷ Accuse no man falsely, but cast aside deception and hypocrisy.

⁸ Slay neither man nor beast for gain or glory, and spill no blood on the altar of pride, for such is the way of the ingrate.

⁹ Bind none to thy will through debt or servitude.

¹⁰ Smite no man in vengeance, yet bear not abuse of thyself or thy neighbor.

¹¹ Steal nothing from thy neighbor, through force, guile or the hand of the king.

¹² Obey no man blindly, as the dog licks the boots of its master, yet pursue wisdom in all things.

¹³ Curse not love, lest she flee from you.

¹⁴ Walk in humility; cast out fear; ask none to bear what you would not.

The Priests

[15] And Osiris appointed three classes of priests to watch over the sons of Adam, charging them to guide and nourish the people in his absence. [16] These men did he leave to care for his garden. And their classes were as follows:

[17] The most worthy among them he called the Elohim, which means "the men who are as gods." To these he granted authority to mediate disputes, to maintain good order and to create such edicts as were good and just for the people. [18] These together convened a council of seventy-two elders which was called The Highest, and he who was chief among them bore the title of Most High.

[19] The second class of priest he named the Cherubim or, in the ancient tongue, Kiribu. Their name meant "mighty protectors," and they were warriors charged with defending the land of Eden. [20] In those days did they wield a sword of flame and fury.

[21] Theirs would be an enduring legacy. In the time of the pharaohs in Egypt, long after the fall of Eden, their order would survive as the Kher-Heb priesthood, and their number was charged with reading out the sacred scrolls in official ceremonies. [22] As the garden's protectors, their symbol was the carob tree, which is preserved in Hebrew lore as the symbol of return. To this day, it bespeaks contentment with one's blessings, which are kept secure by the flaming sword of the Cherubim.

23 The third class of priest was the Seraphim, whose name means "burning serpents." These were the dragonlords of old, the keepers of wisdom and sacred renewal, and the people revered them for their craft and for their cunning. 24 They were masters of herbs and potions that could restore life to the infirm, making them whole again as surely as the serpent itself found new life by shedding its skin.

25 Anyone among the people, man or woman, who studied well and swore an oath to do no harm might join their ranks. And many sought to do so, for no one doubted that they were the wisest among all the people. 26 It is for this reason that one among their number was appointed the guardian of a vineyard that lay in the midst of the garden — the tree of knowledge. This one was Seth, true brother of Osiris.

27 And when he had done these things, Osiris himself departed from them, that he might travel throughout the lands and teach men in all places the way of life, the way of cultivation, of song and music.

28 And men knew nothing of war or of killing.

3

1 When Osiris had gone forth from there, he sojourned long away from Eden. 2 And in time, the Elohim grew bold and haughty, saying to themselves "Our father will never return to us" and "We are the masters of Eden now." 3 Therefore did they take power unto themselves and

reward their favorites with great wealth, neglecting those who did not meet with their approval.

⁴ Seth saw this and was troubled, for it was not his brother's way. And he resolved to go forth beyond Aratta, that he might find Osiris and inform him of these things.

⁵ Leaving another among the Seraphim to guard the tree of knowledge, he set forth boldly with strength of purpose, confident that his quest would bear fruit.

⁶ Over land and sea did he cast his gaze. He searched the slopes of the great mountains, yet he found his brother not. He went to the mouth of the two great rivers, yet discovered no sign of him there. ⁷ South to the land of Sheba did he roam, then also to the mighty Nile, but in neither place did he find Osiris.

⁸ At last, despairing, he returned to Aratta having failed in his purpose, and there was he met with the council of the Elohim.

⁹ "Where have you come from?" the Most High asked of him.

¹⁰ "From roaming throughout the earth, going here and there across the face of it," Seth answered.

¹¹ And the Most High knew of Seth's intention and was pleased that he had failed in his purpose. ¹² Therefore did he taunt him, saying, "Have you considered my servant Job? There is no one in all the earth who is his equal. He walks blameless and upright before me, fearing the Most High and shunning all unrighteousness."

¹³ Now Job was one whom the council had favored because he was loyal to their ways. ¹⁴ To reward him, they

had allotted him livestock numbering more than ten times a thousand. [15] Therefore his family prospered, and his household did flourish. Seven sons and three daughters had come from his loins, and among men he was counted the greatest in all the east. [16] But Seth knew the source of his riches, that it issued forth not from the toil of his hands but instead from council's favor. And he challenged them, scoffing. "Does this one fear you for nothing? Have you not put a hedge around his household and a shield on all he has? [17] You have guaranteed the work of his hands, that nothing may fail him, so that his flocks and his herds spread out across the entire land? But if you were to stretch forth your hand and remove from him this bounty, he will most surely curse you to your face."

[18] And the pride of the Most High was wounded, for he knew that Seth spoke truly, yet he did not dare admit his own connivance. [19] He therefore removed his protection from Job, who at once became afflicted with disease and misfortune. All he had was taken from him. And just as Seth has foretold, curses were found upon his lips.

[20] "The Most High destroys the innocent and the guilty in like manner," he charged. "And if a scourge calls forth death in a moment, he mocks the despair of the blameless."

[21] When these words reached the ears of the Elohim, they were embittered, for they had placed spies among Job's closest friends, men who were as kin to him. And these told the council all the things that they had heard. [22] And the Most High became wroth with Job for his curses, but more so because they had proved the truth of

Seth's accusations. [23]And his words burned into the quick of his marrow and the core of his being, until his pride was wounded and his fury kindled beyond reason.

[24]And he spoke thusly: "Would you annul my justice? Would you condemn me to exonerate yourself?" he shouted. "Is your arm like that of the Most High, and does your voice issue forth like thunder from his mouth? [25] If it be so, then clothe yourself in splendor and glory, and put on the garments of majesty and honor. Send forth the fury of your wrath, that you might bring the proud to their knees and lay the haughty low. [26] Crush those who are, in your esteem, doers of evil. Turn them to dust and consign them to their graves. [27] If you can do these things, then I will heed you and acknowledge that your destiny is your own to command."

[28] Seth heard these things and marveled at the arrogance of the Most High. Yet more than this, he marveled at his folly. [29] By the word of his own mouth, the Most High had proved the case Seth had presented, that Job was no better than any other person, and that he relied altogether on the favor of the council. [30] The Most High, in his conceit, had been forced to admit that he was the source of Job's prosperity and good fortune, just as Seth had argued all along. [31] Yet vindication came at a price for the brother of Osiris and those who, like him, cast their lots with the cause of wisdom. For when the Elohim understood that they had been made sport of, they feared the power of wisdom and of knowledge.

³² Therefore did they seal off the tree of knowledge from all the sons of Adam, placing a fence around it, so that no man could henceforth challenge them by way of greater knowledge. ³³ They forbade any others among the people to join the ranks of the Seraphim, decreeing that none among them should partake of the tree's sweet fruit. ³⁴ "Of every tree in the garden, you may eat your fill," the Most High said in a proclamation. "But in no wise shall you partake of the tree that is in the midst of it, for in the day that you eat from the tree of knowledge — in that day shall you most certainly know death."

4

¹ Seth did not answer the Elohim, neither did he rise up against them. Yet he chafed at their words, and a fire burned within him. ² Taking his own counsel, he said to himself, "How dare these men act as though they were gods! ³ Do they not walk on two legs in the garden like any others? And yet they betray the very spirit of all they were appointed to uphold! ⁴ Did my brother not travel from this place to spread knowledge among the peoples, and would such knowledge then be denied to the people of his own land?"

⁵ He questioned his brother's wisdom in departing, and in appointing the men who had betrayed him. ⁶ And the sons of Adam, in like manner, grew restless, saying, "How long shall we toil for our father who has left us?" ⁷ They awaited his return, but he tarried. And they chafed under

the decrees of the Elohim and beneath the heavy hand of the Cherubim who enforced the council's decrees.

[8] In due course, a woman of their number came to the tree of knowledge and inquired of Seth concerning these matters, for she reasoned that in wisdom she might find the answers to their questions. [9] Then did he speak and say to her: "Did the Most High verily deny you any fruit from this garden he has planted?"

[9] She said to him, "Of the fruit in this garden we may eat, yet from the tree that is in the midst of the garden he has warned us, 'You must not eat from it, or touch it, or you shall know death.'"

[10] But Seth knew that this was not so, and that the Elohim had spread this lie so that members of the council alone should have access to sacred knowledge. [11] "Nay!" he told her. "For the Elohim know that in the day you eat of it, your eyes shall be opened and you will become as they are, knowing good and evil." [12] And when she stepped forward to partake of it, he did not stop her. And when she offered it to her husband, he did not prevent it. [13] But instead did he instruct them in many things concerning knowledge and true wisdom, and they understood what the Elohim had done to them and how those who sat upon the council had, in jealousy, withheld this knowledge for themselves.

[14] Therefore did they pick the fruit of the vine and take it forth unto the winepress. And when the juice from it was fermented, then did they partake of it.

¹⁵ And behold, it came to pass just as Seth had counseled them. They drank a little for inspiration, and seeing it was good, they partook again for folly. And they grew drunk on the strength of the elixir, and they heeded not the decrees of the high council. ¹⁶ But when they came to themselves again their eyes were opened, and they felt naked beneath the heavens, for they knew that their deeds would become known to the Elohim.

¹⁷ None of these things escaped the notice of the Watchers, who gazed down from the master's watchtower. They were witnesses of these events, which are recorded in this chronicle.

¹⁸ And the sons of Adam were no more as children, having dared to challenge the dominion of the Elohim. ¹⁹ It came to pass that the Most High received word of what had happened, and went in search of them. ²⁰ But they heard the sound of him walking in the garden in the cool of the day, and they hid themselves. ²¹ He called out to them, saying, "Where are you?" because he could not find them.

²² After a time, however, they knew they could hide themselves no longer and they came forth and presented themselves to the Most High, saying, "We heard you in the garden and were afraid, knowing that our deeds would be laid bare before you. We felt as naked, fearing punishment, so we hid."

²³ The Most High said to them, "Have you partaken of the tree that is forbidden?"

²⁴ But the two of them, having seen what had befallen Job for his insolence, feared the wrath of the Most High.

[25] And they sought instead to place the blame on Seth, saying, "That serpent Seth deceived us, and we partook."

[26] And the Most High rose up in wrath against each one of them. [27] Full of anger, he directed his fury first at Seth, proclaiming, "Henceforth shall you crawl on your belly before me. Your food shall be dust all the days of your life! [28] No alliance shall you form with the sons of these commoners, for there shall be enmity between you and their offspring. They shall crush your head, and you shall strike at their heels."

[29] Then to the woman who had partaken of the fruit, he declared, "You shall never escape the pains of childbirth. Lust for your husband shall consume you, and he shall subdue you."

[30] And to the man, he said, "The ground shall be cursed on account of you. All the days of your life shall you toil without respite. [31] The ground shall bring forth naught but thistle and briar, and your wages shall be the sweat of your brow. From the ground have you been taken; to the ground you shall return!"

[31] But Seth stood up proudly against the Most High and opposed him to his face, declaring, "Henceforth, I am your adversary! [32] Wisdom shall triumph over folly, and knowledge over base ignorance. No more shall you rule the peoples! [33] In my brother's absence, his duty has become mine. It is your vanity that shall be crushed. Mark my words well, pretender, for they will surely come to pass!"

[34] And Seth gathered to himself those who would oppose the Most High. Among these were many of the

Seraphim, and some also of the Cherubim. [35] But few of the common people joined him, for they trembled before the Most High, who had used the fear of death these many years to keep them in his thrall. [36] When a people is long oppressed, such fear can weave itself into their very being, and so it was with the people of Eden. [37] For Osiris had been so long away that many of them knew no other path but that of submission to the Elohim.

[38] So without them did Seth wage war against the Elohim and their minions for control of Aratta, the Kingdom of Heaven. [39] Seth, the great adversary, fell like lightning from the sky upon his enemies, visiting terrible wrath upon each of them. [40] But the Cherubim struck back with their flaming swords and fiery chariots, trampling the garden beneath them and ruining all that Osiris had planted there, so that it was fallow. [41] And the Most High laughed to himself, saying, "Behold! The curse that I laid upon the sons of Adam has come to pass! The garden is uprooted and fit only for thorns and briars!"

[42] And the two sides fought bitterly, one against the other, yet neither could prevail. [43] The wisdom of Seth and the Seraphim who fought alongside him was great. Yet the soldiers of the Elohim were twice their number. So it was that neither side could gain the advantage. [44] Blood flowed in the rivers that washed down the slopes of Aratta. Smoke from the fires of the warring armies blotted out the very sun. [45] Yet nothing was accomplished. No victory declared. No dispute resolved. Only terror and carnage in battle after battle.

5

¹ Osiris, so long away, was forgotten. Yet he lived still.

² And in the course of time, he sent messengers to collect some of the bounty from his people's harvest, that he might share it upon all the earth. ³ Yet in war, the land had been laid waste. There was no harvest. ⁴ And the Elohim feared that he would discover their poor stewardship of the garden he had left to them, so they waylaid each messenger sent forth to greet them. ⁵ One they beat, and another they killed, and still another they stoned.

⁶ When they failed to return to him, Osiris sent forth still more servants, only to have them dealt with in like manner.

⁷ And the Elohim took counsel among themselves, lamenting, "What if the king himself should return and punish us?"

⁸ But the Most High said to them, "Come, therefore, and let us kill him also."

⁹ And they were sore afraid, saying, "He is a god, and are we not priests sworn to his service?"

¹⁰ Then did the Most High say to them. "Have we not been given the keys to this, the Kingdom of Heaven? ¹¹ See how the people fear us, how they tremble before us. Never did they cower so in the presence of Osiris. ¹² Indeed, our power has surpassed his, and our glory has eclipsed his

fading memory. [13] Am I not the Most High? Do I not sit on the throne of this absent god? And so, have I not become a god in my very being? [14] Verily I say to you that it is so. I am a god, and more: I am a jealous god. These sons of Adam — they shall worship no other god before me. I have sworn it by my own name!"

[15] The others murmured among themselves, but stilled their tongues, for they knew there was danger in this madness.

[16] Then he said to them, "Is it not better that this one die to preserve our position?" And none dared oppose him.

[17] He told them: "No man shall blame us that his life is ended. He has been so long away that few recall his benevolence. [18] And those who would find fault shall cast their gaze upon another: the one who has opposed us from the beginning. For who should inherit the throne of Aratta if not the king's own brother? [19] We shall cast the blame upon him, and none shall dare to question it!"

[20] The council went out from that place, united in their purpose to do as he proposed. They spoke of these things to the Cherubim and counseled them as to what they should say.

[21] And in due course it happened just as the Most High had said it would. [22] At last the king returned to the garden he had planted, and he found it rendered desolate by the war for the Kingdom of Heaven. The fields stood empty and abandoned, and the tree of knowledge had been forsaken. [23] And when he saw this, he searched for his brother, Seth, whom he had charged to tend the tree of

knowledge, but found him not. [24] Yet when he came to the tree of life, and he saw the Cherub priest beside it, Osiris questioned him, saying, "What has happened in this place?"

[25] And the priest told Osiris the words that the man himself had spoken: "That serpent Seth deceived us, and we partook."

[26] Osiris therefore cursed his brother loudly. And he laid a curse also on the tree of knowledge, saying, "No tree can impart true knowledge, which is gained alone from a life lived fully. [27] The knowledge of the vine is fleeting, but the knowledge of struggle endures. And the struggle for Eden shall be its own reward."

[28] So it was that henceforth would the sons of Adam struggle.

[29] As youths they had not known death, yet now would he be their companion. [30] The hyena would stalk them and the vulture would trace their paths across the wastelands. The South Wind would sear their flesh, and the North Wind would howl its contempt for them. [31] No more would the branches of the garden shelter them, but the tents of the wasteland would be their home. [32] As children had they been granted the garden's succor, but their defiance marked them as those who had grown beyond childhood. Yet still they lacked maturity. [33] Their cruelty toward the great king's servants testified against them, and their neglect of the garden condemned them. [34] He knew not that they had acted in the fear of the Elohim, and would not listen to their protests when they sought to speak of it.

[35] Instead did he banish them from the garden he had planted, setting at its entrance a Cherub priest with a flaming sword to guard against their return. [36] And as each man leaves the home of his father at the appointed time, so now they set forth from the garden to make their own way. [37] They went out into the wastelands, enduring each day by their sweat and their sinew. And death hunted them always like a thief at midnight, as it stalks each man at his coming of age.

[38] Seth also went out with them, banished in like manner from the garden under a charge of conspiracy. The barren wastes and red sand deserts became his realm, and his name was changed to Satan, for he had declared, "I am your adversary!" [39] This, too, became the realm of Adam's progeny, for which reason they were called sons of Seth. These were the nomads of old who were called the Hebrew or Habiru, that is, the wanderers. [40] Forgetting the crafts Osiris had taught them, they drifted from place to place across the land, taking their fill of her and passing on to the next place as though she were a harlot.

[41] But the Elohim and those who had stood beside them remained in the land of Aratta, in the heights of the great mountains, the place that would ever be known as the Kingdom of Heaven.

[42] There did they plot out the death of a god.

6

[1] Now Seth was filled with fury at what had been done

to him, but he spoke not of vengeance, remaining ever loyal to his brother's decree.

[2] And the sons of men were, likewise, sorely vexed at their banishment from Eden. "Shall we ever again see the land of our fathers?" they lamented.

[3] And Seth could not answer them, for they had lost faith in his brother and still feared the wrath of the Most High.

[4] So they wandered from that country, pitching their camp at the base of the mountains. And there did they tarry for a time, where they planted a few simple crops and sought to live as best they could in the shadow of their former home. [5] And they bemoaned their lot but found courage in one another, and in their escape from the tyranny of the Elohim. And with this balm did they start to heal.

[6] Such was their state when an emissary from Aratta came to them from out of the mountains one day. And they knew him to be one of the Malachim, the angels who were official messengers of the Elohim. [7] He came to them from the council of the seventy-two, bearing greetings with the words, "Peace! Peace!" [8] And he said to them, "The Most High has forgiven your trespass, and you have been summoned to return by his good pleasure. For the Most High has prepared a feast to honor Osiris, and all the people have been called to join him."

[9] At this did the sons of Adam rejoice, for though they feared the Elohim, they longed to see their home again.

[10] Seth, too, had been summoned. And though he was

loath to trust a Malach of the Elohim, even so he sought to be reconciled with his brother. [11] Therefore did he accompany the sons of Adam back to Eden, unaware of the intrigues that his enemies had prepared against him.

[12] For the Most High had devised a scheme to supplant Osiris on the throne. And with the seventy-two as his co-conspirators, he set the plot in motion. [13] The artifice unfolded in this manner: The council crafted for themselves a large ark of the finest wood, covered in gold and precious jewels, and waited until the day of the great feast they had prepared. [14] Then, when all the people had gathered to pay tribute to Osiris, the Most High presented this ark before the entire company, saying, "This is the gift of the wise Seth to this assembly, in tribute to his brother!" [15] Yet Seth knew nothing of this, and when he opened his mouth to protest, the words were lost amid the murmurs of the crowd.

[16] And the Most High spoke up once more, presenting to the guests this challenge: "Whosoever shall fit inside the box perfectly shall then claim it as his own!"

[17] Now the Elohim had so fashioned the box that none save Osiris would be able to enter it. So each of the guests stepped forward one by one, but none was able to meet the challenge. [18] Then at length did the turn pass to Osiris, and so he climbed inside and found it fit him perfectly! [19] But at that same moment, men in service to the Elohim rushed forward to seal the ark while the king reclined there. They poured molten metals over the lid to hold it fast. [20] And with great alacrity did they make their escape, shouting,

"Glory to Seth, the true king!" though they served not Seth but his enemies, who would have him faulted for the death of his brother.

²¹ These men spirited the ark away from the assembly, but Queen Isis followed them in haste.

²² And the servants of the Elohim took it many miles across the land, down from the mountains and over the plains between the waters; through the deserts and down into the heart of Egypt. ²³ And there did they cast off the ark containing the mummy of the fallen king, Osiris, thinking at last they would be rid of him in this land so far from Eden.

²⁴ But the queen was diligent in her quest to recover his body, and after a long search came upon the ark at last. A tamarisk tree had grown up around it, preserving it from wind and rain, sun and storm. ²⁵ When she opened it, she saw her beloved reposed as if in sleep, and in joy set forth to return him again to his homeland. ²⁶ Yet still did the servants of the Elohim wait silent in the shadows, among the reeds beside the river. And as the queen slept, they came in stealth to open the ark. ²⁷ And they cut the king's body into many pieces, which they scattered across all the land.

²⁸ When Isis discovered what had befallen her king-husband, she cried out to all the gods in lamentation. ²⁹ She called to her sister Nephthys, who was also the wife of Seth, so that they together scoured the land from marsh to desert in search of the king's lost body. ³⁰ And Seth himself did aid them, though he dared not show his face, for the

blame for his brother's demise had been cast now squarely upon his shoulders. Yet he helped them from the shadows and he assisted from the shelter of the rushes along the Nile. [31] To this task did they dedicate themselves for many years. And when at last they had gathered the pieces, Isis assembled them anew and wrapped them in linen cloths. [32] Breathing her healing magic upon Osiris, she restored him in a moment, and in that moment conceived a child by him in spirit. This was Horus of the Horizon.

[33] And when Horus had grown to manhood, he became the king of Egypt. His sign is the falcon and the fiery sun, for which reason he also bears the nature of the mystical bird that is called the phoenix. [34] In his honor do the kings of Egypt adorn themselves with the name of Horus, and when they pass from the realm of men they are honored as Osiris. [35] But Osiris himself ascended to the highest of heavens, whence he had come; to the heights above Aratta, so that he was found no more among them. [36] But some said he could be seen among the stars drawing back his bow there. And they called him also Anu, after the heavens themselves, for he became the lord of heaven, whence he reigned supreme over all he did survey.

[37] And Seth withdrew to the shadowy places, where he took refuge from the lies that were spread against him. [38] From time to time would he emerge to face derision, scorn and mockery from the sons of Adam who had shared his fate. [39] For the Elohim, having accomplished their purpose in destroying the king of heaven, did once more cast the sons of Adam out of Eden, saying, "Your seed is

tainted by evil from now to eternity, for you have followed the way of Seth, the father or lies and deception!"

[40] Therefore did the Elohim claim Eden for themselves, and rule there over the host of their minions.

7

[1] But those who had been exiled from the Kingdom of Heaven chose one from among them as their king. This one was a fisherman called Adam, after their tribe, and he took to wife a maid who was found in the wastelands. [2] This one was Lilith, "the breath of the moon," who came to him in the night on the South Wind and who was the queen of heaven in the guise of a maiden. [3] She bore to him two heirs, who became the first great rulers among the race of men. The first of these was Cain, whose name means "king" and "conqueror," and the second was A'bel, whose name, rendered elsewhere as Ba'al, means "lord."

[4] But there arose a dispute between Adam and Lilith, for he demanded that she submit and lie beneath him. She, however, refused him and departed to the shadows. [5] To this day is Lilith's scorn heard to echo across the wastes and canyons. Hers is the voice of the night owl who flies solitary, casting shadows on the moon. [6] Even still she submits to no man, but guards with jealous eyes her wisdom.

[7] For this purpose is a veil drawn full across woman's countenance, that it might be hidden from the sons of men

until the bridal chamber. [8] This is not done for modesty, as the sons of men in their wounded pride falsely claim. But it is done after the manner Lilith, who hid herself from proud Adam rather than be made his servant. [9] As the veil of darkness is drawn across the moon, so it is with the veil of this mystery. And no man may remove it, but each woman has it in her choosing to wear or reject it.

[10] He who has ears to hear, let him hear.

[11] Now Cain remembered the ways of Osiris and planted for himself fields of grain to harvest, but A'bel was a nomad like his father and a wanderer tending flocks and herds. [12] It was in those days that men began to sacrifice to the gods, hoping to gain their favor. Cain therefore offered up a sacrifice of the fruits of his labors, but A'bel brought forth a sacrifice of from among his flocks. [13] For the first time then was blood spilled out upon the earth, and the gods were grieved that it was so.

[14] But Cain, seeing what his brother had done, thought that the gods had approved this thing. [15] Therefore did he come upon his brother in the fields and slay him, reasoning that the blood of a man would be all the more pleasing to heaven. [16] At this, however, the gods were sore afflicted, for blood begets blood, and vengeance begets vengeance. Death begets death, and hardship begets hardship. Once the cycle is begun, men are hard-pressed to break it.

[17] For this reason did the gods send Cain forth with a mark upon his flesh, that no man might do violence against him for the deed that he had done, lest he be avenged sevenfold. [18] And they banished him from the fields that he

had planted, casting him out into the land of Nod, which means "wandering." [19] So it was that he became a wanderer like the brother he had slain, and he came down out of the mountains into Shinar beside the mighty Euphrates. [20] For this reason is it said that in those days, the kingship came down out of heaven, for it descended with Cain who had been king.

[21] And Cain lay with his wife, and she gave birth to a son, who was called Enoch.

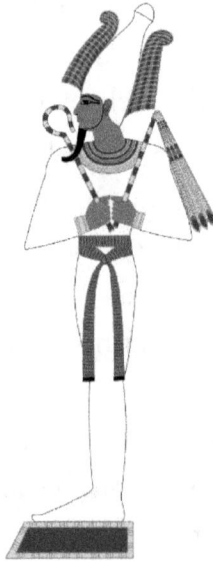

The Book of

Babylon

1

¹ This is the book of Babylon, the land between the rivers, which is at the center of the Earth. It is the book of Enoch and Etana, of Ur and of Eridu. Therein lies the gate of the gods.

² Enoch came first to this place from Aratta. He was strong of mind and heart, and he set forth to build for

himself a dwelling place in Shinar near the southern sea, which was the first great city in all the land. ³ He named it Irad or Eridu, which means "a place far away," for it was far from the garden that his forebears left behind. ⁴ For this reason was he called the father of Irad, because he laid its foundation stone.

⁵ For its placement, he chose the marshlands near the mouth of the great Euphrates, where the sweet waters of the abyss rise up from beneath the earth to join the bitter waters of the stormy sea. ⁶ Enoch was lord of the sweet waters, which nourished the land and the people round about.

⁷ So it was that when kingship descended from Aratta, it came upon Eridu, and Enoch, heir to the throne of Cain, was the first to rule. The people called him Enki, which means "lord of the land," after the lord of the earth in Aratta. ⁸ He built for himself a habitation which rose above the city, and was magnificent in all its aspects. ⁹ So was it written of his dwelling place:

> Enki the Lord who decrees the fates
> Built his house of silver and lapis lazuli,
> Like sparkling light.
> The pure house he built
> He adorned lavishly with gold.

> ¹⁰ In Eridu he built the house of water-bank,
> Its brickwork speaking words of wisdom,
> Like an ox roaring,

The house of Enki gives voice to his oracles.

[12] Indeed did he rule in wisdom and in power. He walked with the gods and wrote down their ways on many tablets, which he called the ME. Some say he inscribed them in precious emerald, and others on bricks of clay. [13] It was he who wrote down the ways of the gods for the generations of men to remember, setting forth sixty-four decrees for them to follow. [14] Among these were the way of power and the way of wisdom, the way of peace and the way of judgment, the way of the bridechamber and the way the throne. [15] Taking reed stylus in hand, he set forth, too, the way of the shepherd and the way of the divine lady, and also the ways of many musical instruments. And also did he leave instruction concerning the rivers, should they rise over their banks and flood the earth.

[16] Casting his eyes to the heavens did he study the ways of the Watchers until he learned them all according to their order, committing every detail of the sky's secrets to writing, that men might know the seasons of the year and their progressions. [17] From far and wide men came to hear his wisdom, which he shared with them freely, as a father shares bounty with his children. He taught them, as Osiris had before him:

[18] "The sun rises in six portals and sets in six portals, as also does the moon. And the leaders of the stars also, six in the east and six others in the west, follow one after the other in orderly fashion. [19] First goes forth the great luminary called the sun, whose face is like the face of

heaven, yet full of a fire that sends forth heat and brilliance. [20] The wind drives the chariot on which he rises, and he descends in from the heavens toward the north that he might find a haven in the east."

[21] "The moon is a circle like the fields of heaven, and the wind drives the chariot upon which she rides. Her light does she impart in varied measure, waxing and again waning with each new month. [22] Her days are like those of the sun, and her head faces in an easterly manner when, on the thirtieth day, she is manifested."

[23] So great was Enki's wisdom that it was said of him:

When Enki rises, the fish rise,
The abyss stands in wonder,
Joy enters into the sea,

[24] Fear comes over the deep,
Terror holds the exalted river,
The Euphrates, the South Wind lifts it in waves.

[25] And the people likewise built dwellings of reed and mud-brick. From the earth they dug canals to water their cropland, and they made square boats called arks to bear them across the land. [26] And Enoch's grandfather Adam came down from Aratta, near bountiful Eden whence he had been banished, and ruled with him at his side. [27] He was the first of seven sages in the time before the flood who served as counselors to seven great kings. These men were the Annunaki, mighty men of old who came down

from heaven to dwell upon the earth. ²⁸ They came down from Aratta and took the daughters of Shinar to wife, and made alliance with them.

²⁹ They are called by some the Nephilim and called Lugal, which means "giant" or "big man."

2

¹ Adam the fisherman fashioned for himself the vestments of a sage, which were sewn in the shape of a fish. So it appeared he had the head of a man but also of a great sea creature as his crown, along with the scales of its back upon his own. ² And he came forth by day to teach the people of Eridu the ways of heaven, whence he had come, but each night he withdrew to the ocean and plied his trade among the waves.

³ As it is written:

His word commands
Like the word of the gods
Who granted him wisdom to reveal the way of the land
To him is given wisdom
Yet not eternal life
A sage, no one rejects his word

⁴ He bakes with the bakers
Preparing food and water for Eridu by day
He sets the table with pure hands

And plies the waters in his boat
He does the fishing for Eridu

⁵ One night, he embarked in his sailing boat to bring forth fish for the good of Eridu. Without a rudder, his boat would drift. Without a steering pole would he set forth.

⁶ Now Lilith, who had spurned him, had not forgotten his mistreatment. Though he had beckoned her, she had not returned to him, but had stored up her anger for the appropriate time. ⁷ So it was that on this evening, she sent forth the South Wind to punish him, and it overturned the sailing vessel from which he was fishing. ⁸ Therefore in his wrath did Adam curse the South Wind, boasting, "I shall break your wing!" And in the moment that he said it, the South Wind's wing was broken, so that for seven days it did not blow toward the land.

⁹ It therefore came to pass that he was called to account by the gods, and he was summoned to Eden in the highlands to explain his actions.

¹⁰ But Adam was anxious for his welfare, and he knew not what awaited him in Aratta, from which place he had been cast out once before. ¹¹ Would Osiris judge him again from the highest heaven as Anu? Would he be consigned to the abyss beneath the earth?

¹² So did Enoch offer counsel, that he should flatter the sentinels at Eden's gate, saying, "They will speak in your favor."

¹³ But he warned him, "They will hold out the bread of death for you, so you must not eat. And they will offer you

the water of death, so you must not drink. [14] Only adorn yourself with the garment that they give you and anoint yourself with the oil they provide. [15] Neglect not the instructions I have given you, and keep to the words I have told you."

[16] After a time did an envoy arrive from Aratta and accompanied Adam up to the heavens. [17] When he arrived at the gates did he repeat the words of Enoch to the sentinels, who spoke out in his favor so that Osiris was appeased. [18] And he spread forth his hands and asked them, "What shall we do for this one? Fetch him the bread of life eternal and allow him to partake!"

[19] Yet Adam recalled when Osiris had cast him out from Eden, withholding life eternal from him. And he remembered his offense against the South Wind and the warning that Enoch had given. [20] Surely he could not have been so easily forgiven. Surely this was a trick, that he might taste the bread of death.

[21] So when they fetched him the bread of life, he would not eat.

[22] And when they brought him the water of life he would not drink.

[23] They brought him a garment, and he put it on himself.

[24] They fetched him oil, and he anointed himself.

[25] So was he made fit for burial, in the manner of all the great kings throughout the ages. [26] Once they pass from this world, no more do they eat. [27] Once they pass from this lifetime, no more do they drink. [28] But they are anointed

with balm and adorned with white cloth for their passage to the world to come. And they are seen no more.

29 Therefore did Osiris question him, saying, "Why did you not eat? Why did you not drink? Do you not wish to be immortal? 30 Take him, therefore, and send him back into the earth from which he came."

31 So it was that the mystery of the bread and the cup continued, and men partook in the hope of eternal life. But Adam's body was prepared for burial, and Enoch saw him no more. 32 Still, it is said that he came to Eridu a shade, no longer eating and drinking but teaching the men there all the secrets he had learned in Eden.

33 It is written:

He would pass the day among men
But took no food in that season
He gave them insight into letters and science
And art of every kind

34 He taught them to build cities
And to found temples
To compile laws
And the way of shapes and patterns

35 He taught them to distinguish the seeds of earth
And showed them how to collect fruits
And he instructed them in all things
To ease their manner and give them reason

³⁶ Since then nothing has been added
To improve his instruction
And when the sun set, he retired to the sea once more
And passed the night in the deep

3

¹ Enoch mourned the passing of his grandfather, and sought to return likewise to the land from which he had come. ² When therefore all things that had been appointed to him were accomplished, the gods sent forth the chariot of the sun to greet him. ³ And he returned to the land of the heavens, to Eden, as Osiris had done before him. ⁴ There did he accept the bread of life which Adam had refused at his bidding. ⁵ He inscribed the wisdom of the ages from which the race of men would turn away, and so became known as Enoch the scribe, the heavenly chronicler. And the Watchers did his bidding.

⁶ Now it came to pass that other cities rose up with their kings to rival Eridu, and the kingship passed from one to the next over the course of many years. ⁷ Two kings ruled from the throne of Enki before the scepter passed to the coppersmiths to the north in Bad-Tabira, at the edge of the marshlands.

⁸ After this, the kingship passed to Larak, on the right hand of the Euphrates between Eridu and Bad-Tabira, and thence to Sippar, upstream many leagues to the north. ⁹ This was the "city of the birds," a place of trade whence goods were shipped down the great river to the cities and

fields below, a way station between the rich mountain highlands of Aratta and the river plains of Shinar.

[10] And when the kingship passed from Sippar, it came at last to Shuruppak, the "place of healing" along the Euphrates. Here two kings did reign.

[11] The first of them, named Lamech, took to himself two wives, whose names were Adah and Zillah, and they bore him many sons. [12] Adah gave birth to Jabal the herdsman and also Jubal, master of the flute. [13] Zillah bore him Tubal-Cain, a master forger of bronze and iron who dwelt in Bad-Tabira, and a daughter, Naamah.

[14] But there was strife in Shuruppak, and a young man entered into the presence of Lamech to assail him, wounding him. [15] Lamech, however, slew him in his own defense. [16] After these things had come to pass, he called his wives to him, saying, "Adah and Zillah, hearken to me; wives of Lamech, attend my voice. I have slain a man for wounding me, a young man for doing me violence." [17] therefore issued a warning to any man who would seek to do him violence, that the gods would avenge him: "If Cain is avenged seven times," he declared, "then Lamech seventy times seven."

[18] After this he sired another son, who would become his heir. [19] The newborn's body was white as snow and red as the blooming of a rose, and the hair of his head and his long locks were white as wool, and his eyes beautiful. When he opened them, his radiant joy lit up the whole house like the sun. [20] His appearance was a source of great hope to the king, whose land had long been plagued by drought and

famine. [21] It is written:

> When the second year arrived,
> The storehouse was depleted
> [22] When the third year arrived,
> Men's faces showed starvation
>
> [23] When the fourth year arrived,
> Their proud bearing was downcast
> [24] Their well-set shoulders slouched
> They went in public hunched over
>
> [25] When the fifth year arrived,
> A daughter would see her mother coming in
> A mother would not so much as open the gates to greet
> her daughter
>
> [26] When the sixth year arrived,
> They served a daughter for a meal
> They served a son for nourishment

[27] It was in these days that Lamech's son was conceived. And he named the child Noah, which means "comforter," for he said, "This one will comfort us amidst the afflictions of our toil, for our hands labor in vain to till the soil that has been cursed of the gods."
[28] For the gods had grown weary of the ways of men, and the din of their boasting was deafening as they made war one with another. [29] They took the names of the gods

in vain, claiming their sanction on war and violence. And no sooner did one city lay claim to the scepter of kingship than another assailed it, besieging its walls and denying it the earth's bounty for the sake of dominion. [30] These were the ways of the lowland cities, and the gods feared that should they continue, the sons of men might presume even to attack Aratta.

4

[1] Noah ruled wisely and soothed Shuruppak with the balm of peace. [2] He prospered in his kingdom, and as his years advanced, he increased in wisdom, so that his people called him Ziusudra, the long-lived one, and Atra-Hasis, which means "exceedingly wise." [3] He took the sacred tablets of his forefather, Enoch, and consulted them in all things. And when he watched the heavens, he saw the clouds begin to gather. [4] When he cast his eyes to the earth, he saw the wells spring up and the Euphrates overflow its banks. [5] And he knew that the gods had grown wroth with the men of the lowlands, but knew not what to do.

[6] So he took refuge in his reed hut and hearkened to the words that Enoch had written on the sacred tablets in days long past, in the tablet of the flood. It was as though he spoke to Noah through the very walls of his hut. [7] And he counseled him on the things that he must do. [8] Should the gods lament the ways of man and bring destruction upon them in the form of water, these actions should he take:

[9] Tear down your house and build an ark
Abandon your goods and seek after life
[10] Forswear belongings, but preserve your soul
Aboard this vessel take the seed of all things living

[11] Build for her a covering
That the sun may not see inside her
Let her be covered, fore and aft
[12] The rigging must be firm
And the bitumen be strong!

[13] So Noah did as Enoch bade him. He found the falcon and the osprey, the owl and the vulture. [14] He brought to him oxen and asses, cattle and swine, goats and sheep, the gazelle and the dromedary. [15] He built for himself an ark to house his flocks and herds, and all the animals that lived upon his lands. [16] In it also he placed the sacred tablets, so that they might be preserved amid the destruction. [17] So it came to pass that the tablets thenceforth would be housed within an ark, a vessel to protect them for his children and their children, the heirs to the wisdom of Enoch.

[18] And when he had prepared everything as Enoch had commanded him, he gave a feast for all the people, and invited them to partake. But Noah could neither eat nor be still, for he feared the deluge that was to come. [19] Whilst all the others ate their fill, Noah's heart was torn and bile rose up from his inward parts.

[20] And in that moment, the face of the heavens changed, and the thunderer bellowed from on high. [21] Noah called for bitumen and sealed the ark's door shut. He cut the rope that held the vessel fast. [22] And in this very moment the winds did rage, and the bird of heaven, Anzu, tore at the sky with his talons.

[23] The flood burst forth upon them like an army attacking. Eyesight was vanquished, and the skies were black as night. [24] The deluge roared like a bull in fury, and the winds howled like a wild ass screaming. [25] The Tigris was swollen like a womb awaiting childbirth, and the Euphrates overflowed its banks from Sippar to Eridu. [26] The heavens opened up and crashed down mightily on the land, as wells sprang up from the abyss. [27] Great cities were inundated, the crops of the field were ruined, and the sea rose up to devour the marshes. [28] Such was the fury of it that it seemed the entire earth might be swallowed, for the clouds filled the heavens as far as the eye could see.

[29] Like dragonflies, the bodies of men filled up the river. Like a raft they moved the edge of the boat.

[30] And the storm was upon them many days and nights. It did not abate, nor did it falter, until finally the gods were appeased in their anger. [31] The sun shone forth once more, and clouds were driven from the face of heaven; at night the stars were seen again, and the moon shone forth in pale brilliance. [32] Only then did Noah venture forth from within the ark. [33] He sent forth a raven, which flew to and fro until the waters had receded. Then he sent forth a dove, but it returned to him, and so he waited seven days before he

sent it forth again. [34] Then did it go out from him and return to him come evening with an olive branch, newly plucked, within its beak. [35] By this did he know that the flood had not destroyed all things within the river valley, but that some life was preserved.

[36] Yet when Noah surveyed the land, he saw that the waters had claimed every field of the lowlands. [37] The roads and the byways were now as canals, the pastures were as lakes, and the cities belonged to the watery abyss. [38] But when he cast his eyes to the far-distant highlands, they fell upon the peaks of Aratta, which rose up proudly above the waters all around him, and he thought, "This is where the dove found haven." [39] So he released it yet again and went after it, and the ark journeyed forth until it reached the base of the mountains, where the waters could not follow.

[40] Then he climbed up until he reached Eden, the great plain in the land of Aratta whence his fathers had come. [41] He climbed the mountains of the gods and built in that place an altar, for he said to himself, "The waters shall not rise to this land of heaven, therefore shall it be preserved should a flood again come upon us." [42] And he set the sacred tablets of his forefather Enoch on the altar there, within an ark, for which reason it is said that the ark came to rest upon the mountains of Aratta.

[43] And the men of Shinar remembered this, and they held it in their hearts.

[44] And the gods made a covenant with Noah never again to flood the land with such a deluge, saying:

As long as the earth endures
In seed time and in harvest
In cold and in heat
In summer and winter
Day and night shall never cease

[45] They pledged then no more to do violence to the sons of men, and the great archer of heaven so declared it: "This is the sign of the covenant we affirm with you, and with every creature for all generations." [46] And Osiris, the great archer of the heavens, set his bow upon the clouds; it was a bow of many colors for the many shades of life, from those who dwell in Shinar to the sons and daughters of Aratta, and for all things that draw breath or take root within the earth.

5

[1] Noah planted a vineyard there in Eden, for he wished to restore the tree of knowledge. Yet he understood not the way of the vine, and in his greed drank too much of its harvest. [2] When, therefore, his sons came upon him, they found him naked and began to quarrel amongst themselves, until their disputes reached the ears of the Elohim. [3] And the Most High said to his brethren, "Shall we yet again abide these fools? Nay, let us be rid of them! For they are wicked sons of Adam, bearing within themselves the very seed of iniquity!"

⁴ Therefore did the Most High speak lies to the sons of Noah and cause their hearts to be hardened against one another in enmity. ⁵ Then did they part ways from one another, removing themselves to the ends of the earth so that Ham traveled southward to Egypt and beyond, while Japheth sojourned among the Greeks and Scythians. ⁶ But Shem took for his portion the land beneath Aratta, whence his father had come, and his people were called the Shemites.

⁶ And the sons of Shem were close by the black-headed people of the river delta, who had abode in Shinar since ancient times.

⁷ Now the lowlands were destitute, and few men still dwelt there. But when the waters receded and the rivers withdrew again to their appointed courses, the fields blossomed and the land again became fertile. ⁸ Then did men multiply once more upon the earth, increasing their flocks and their herds alongside them. ⁹ So it was that the kingship descended from heaven a second time, and it came to the city of Kish, which some call Cush. ¹⁰ This was a mighty city, with walls and battlements. Such was its fame and glory that thenceforth did all the kings of Shinar take to themselves the title King of Kish.

¹¹ And their kings demanded worship like the gods, after the manner of the Elohim. They claimed Inanna herself as their consort, and appointed their sons to bear the scepter at their passing. ¹² So it was with the kings of Kish. And the greatest of these was Etana.

¹³ The star queen descended from heaven
In search of a shepherd
She sought a king across the lands

¹⁴ Inanna came down out of heaven
In search of a shepherd
She sought a king to rule them

¹⁵ And the Lord of the Air measured the dais of Etana
Whom the star queen loved steadfastly
And so he decreed

¹⁶ "She has sought for herself a shepherd
Let kingship be upon the land
May the heart of Kish be joyful
At kingship, the radiant crown, the throne of splendor."

¹⁷ For this reason kings are called shepherds to this day,
and the pharaoh takes to himself the shepherd's crook as a
sign of authority, and Etana was henceforth called "The
Shepherd."

6

¹ Etana ruled the land for many years, yet had no heir,
and for this reason was he greatly troubled. ² He wished
therefore to procure for himself the plant of birthing,
which only grew in the heights of heaven, in the highlands
of Aratta. ³ For this was the place of his fathers' fathers, the

land of beginnings where the gods still dwelt. Surely, he reasoned, they would impart to him the plant of birthing.

⁴ And in a reverie, this dream came to Etana. ⁵ He saw himself building a tower to heaven, which he named High Water, and in the shade of it grew a poplar tree. ⁶ In its crown of this tree an eagle settled, and a serpent at its root. ⁷ The eagle said to the serpent, "Come, let us make ourselves a friendship. Let us be comrades, you and I!" ⁸ This pleased the serpent, so they made a pact between themselves to share the food of all the land. ⁹ They would go forth together toward the mountains, and there would the eagle hunt gazelle and wild oxen, whereupon he would bring this bounty to the serpent and its offspring. ¹⁰ In like manner would the serpent go forth and hunt the beasts of the field, and return with them as an offering for the eagle's nest.

¹¹ Because of this, the eagle's children flourished and grew strong. ¹² And before long, the eagle became bold and said to himself, "I do not need the serpent, but in my own strength shall prosper!" ¹³ He therefore plotted against his ally, saying, "I shall eat the sons of the serpent. The serpent I shall betray! And I shall ascend to heaven like the gods!"

¹⁴ Now the smallest of his fledglings, who was exceedingly wise, counseled him not to pursue these ends, lest he incur the wrath of the sun god. ¹⁵ But he hearkened not to this warning, neither did he heed the words of his offspring, but determined in his heart to carry out his evil purpose. ¹⁶ And when the serpent went forth did the eagle

assail his nest, and when the serpent was gone did he devour his young.

[17] When the serpent returned from the hunt, bearing his burdens, he cast them down at the foot of the poplar and looked about him. [18] Behold, his nest was gone! Behold, his children were no more! [19] The eagle had gouged the ground with his talon, and a cloud of dust rose up toward heaven.

[20] The serpent wept. And the sun god, the god of enlightenment, counseled him.

[21] Then did he plot revenge against the eagle, and he laid an ambush for his betrayer. [22] He hid himself inside the carcass of an ox, and when the eagle came forth to partake of it, he sprang upon him. [23] He clipped his wings and plucked his pinions, and cast him down from his nest into a pit from which he could not escape. [24] And the eagle screeched in protest, so that his voice reached the ears of Etana.

[25] And he thought, if he did befriend the eagle and free him from his prison, perhaps the great bird would bear him up to the heavens on its wings!

[26] So Etana took the eagle by the hand and lifted him up out of the pit, whereupon he took food like a ravening lion. And gaining strength, he said to Etana, "Let us be friends, you and I. Ask me whatsoever you may desire, and I shall grant it."

[27] Therefore did Etana make known the desires of his heart, and the eagle agreed to bear him up into the heavens, that he might procure the plant of birthing. [28] The eagle spoke thus to Etana, "By the grace of Inanna, place your

arms against my sides. Place your hands upon my wing feathers, and let us now ascend!"

²⁹ And when he had borne Etana aloft one league, he said to him, "Look, my friend, how the land is now! It is as a circle one-fifth its size, and the sea is as a paddock."

³⁰ And when he had borne him aloft a second league, he said to him, "Look, my friend, how the land is now! It has become as a garden, and the vast sea has become as a trough."

³¹ And when he had borne him aloft a third league, he said to him, "Look, my friend, how the land is now!"

³² But Etana could not see the land, nor could his eyes behold the vast sea far below. And he reconsidered going farther up to heaven, and he entreated the eagle to set him down and let him return again to his city. ³³ One league did the eagle drop him down, then plunged to catch him on his wings. ³⁴ A second league did the eagle drop him down, then plunged to catch him on his wings. ³⁵ And a third league did the eagle drop him down, then plunged to catch him on his wings, until at last he returned to the city whence he had come.

³⁵ Waking from his reverie, Etana wondered, and he sought out the meaning of this dream. ³⁶ This is its interpretation: The eagle was a ruler of the people, who in his pride betrayed an alliance with the serpent. And these two made war, one with the other, because the serpent sought to cast down the eagle from his lofty perch.

³⁷ Now would the eagle, in his zeal, seek for himself an alliance with Etana, that together they might defend the

heavens against the serpent's scions. ³⁸ And Etana would agree to these things, on condition that he be given the plant of birthing, which is a shoot from the tree of life.

³⁹ Because of these things, Etana made peace with the land of Aratta and obtained the plant of birthing, whereupon his wife conceived and gave birth to an heir, Balih. In this manner was the royal line was preserved in Kish.

⁴⁰ So Aratta and Kish remained at peace, and Etana entered into his rest. And ten more kings ruled after him, until at last Eanna went out to battle against Kish and defeated her, and the kingship was carried off to Eanna. ⁴¹ And though the Elohim yet ruled in Aratta, their time of lordship there was drawing to a close, for soon would there arise a king who would challenge the very gates of heaven and prevail.

7

¹ As the world has its ages, so does also the race of man, whose epochs are marked at the gates of the stars.

² The first of these is the age of the lion, during which the great sphinx of Egypt arose. This was the golden age when the tides rose up from their sea beds and the desert sands washed new across the lands called Libya.

³ The second is the age of the protector, whose shell is hardened and whose mistress is the moon. This was the age when man dwelt in the protection of the gods, in the place between land and sea.

⁴ The third is the age of the partners, who stretch forth their hands to one another in homage to their likeness. It was in this age that the sons of the earth joined together in the first great enterprises, and they mastered the crops of the field.

⁵ The fourth is the age of the bull, the age of bronze, in which the sons of men did harness the beasts of the land, placing yokes upon their necks and mounting them in conquest. In this way did they greatly expand their dominion. And they began sacrificing animals on their altars to please the gods, for which the gods turned away from them.

⁶ The fifth is the age of the ram on the mountain cliff, when the bull was slain in violence. And men did seek to reach the heights of heaven but were cast down again in shame. ⁷ This was the age of iron, when great armies fought like rams for land and glory. And all men trembled before them as they invoked the names of their gods. Yet still the gods forsook them.

⁷ The sixth is the age of the oceanborn, when men shall seek the depths of their own souls, yet find them not amidst the rancor. And the gods shall speak, but men shall not have ears to hear.

⁸ The seventh is the age of the water bearer, when the heavens and the earth shall be reconciled, and the sons of men shall once more know the gods.

⁹ He who has ears to hear, let him hear.

¹⁰ In the age of Eanna, men exalted the bull god who raged in the heavens and raised banners to wage war like

beasts that trample down the earth. [11] They turned away from the sun god who gives light from on high and, bent on conquest, they knelt before the storm god who thunders from heaven. [12] As a bellowing ox, he does violence to the land. As a mighty dragon, he casts fire upon the earth.

[13] This was the age of mighty cities and great warriors, the hunter kings who subdued the land. [14] The greatest of these cities was Eanna, and the greatest of these kings was Enmr-Kar, whose name means Nimrod the Hunter.

[15] He placed on his head the horns of the bull god, and with his armies subdued the land between the rivers. [16] He took for himself Babel and Akkad, and other cities across Shinar. And thence he went forth to Assur and built up Nineveh as his own. Yet his throne was in Eanna, the "House of Heaven" by the banks of the Euphrates.

[17] There did he build the great city of Unuq, which he named for his ancestor Enoch. Those who dwelt there were the Anakim, the sons of Enoch whom some men knew as Anak. [18] And Enmr-Kar built a wall around this place so as to enclose it for a vast distance and secure it against his enemies. [19] But his crowning glory was to be in the midst of the cities, wherein he sought to build anew the tree of life that was in Eden, a great new watchtower as a tribute to the goddess queen of heaven, whose name is Isis and Inanna. [20] This tower he built as a ladder and a mountain, with steps carved into the sides of it that the sons of men might ascend to the heavens.

[21] For he said to himself, "The gods are safe in their heavens. Now what if they should forget their promise, and

again unleash the waters of the abyss upon this land?
²² Therefore shall we become like the gods and build a place of refuge, that we may ascend the stairway to heaven and commune with them."

²³ This place would be nothing less than a new dwelling place for Inanna. Adorned with all the finest jewels and every precious metal, it would be a gateway for the gods between the heavens and the earth.

²⁴ Therefore did he name this place Babilim, which means "Gate of the Gods."

²⁵ Enmr-Kar boasted that no more would the sons of men pine for Aratta, for he would make a new heaven and new earth in Unuq. ²⁶ And Innana would come down from the highlands to dwell among them, forsaking her abode in the land of Eden. ²⁷ So he besought Inanna, saying:

Let Aratta fashion gold and silver skilfuflly
On my behalf, for the sake of Unuq
²⁸ Let them cut lapis lazuli without flaw from the blocks
That I may build a holy mountain in Unuq

²⁹ Let Aratta build a temple brought down from heaven
Let Aratta fashion your abode
³⁰ Let Aratta submit beneath the yoke of Unuq
On my behalf

³¹ Let the people of Aratta bring down stones from the mountain
To build a great shrine

Erect the great abode
The abode of the gods

[32] Make the abyss rise up for me like a shining mountain
Make Eridu gleam like the range of mountains
[33] May the abyss shine forth like silver from the lode
I shall bring the ME from Eridu

[34] When I am adorned with the crown of lordship
Like a purified shrine
[35] When I place upon my head
The crown of Unuq Kulaba
[36] And the people shall marvel
With the sun god as my witness
In my joy

[37] Yet Inanna scorned his advances, for would any temple made with human hands be wondrous enough to contain her majesty? Not she, the queen of heaven, whose canopy was the night sky and whose doorposts were the tall cedars. [38] Enmr-Kar sought to woo her and, by subtlety, entrance her. Yet the subtlety of men is like a clamorous gong to the ears of a goddess. [39] So she spurned him, though he did not know it, and she rebuffed it, though he would not accept it. [40] For the declaration of a goddess is like a whisper to the ears of proud men, who wage war in the name of the heavens and defile the names of the gods with their folly.

8

[1] When he was convinced that he had received the blessing of Inanna (though he knew not the truth, that she had scorned him), Enmr-Kar called to himself a messenger to make an embassy to Aratta and give word to the lord of that land what was required of him. [2] "Let Aratta pack nuggets of gold in leather sacks," he said. [3] "Place alongside it the kumea ore. Package up also precious metals, and load the packs on the donkeys of the mountains"

[4] He sent him also with this word of warning, should the lord of Aratta defy him, that he would make people fly forth from that city like a dove from the bough of a tree, and that it would gather dust like a city utterly ruined.

[5] So the messenger went forth from there. He journeyed by the starry night and traveled by day with the sun of heaven. [6] He brought his message up into the highlands and descended with it from the highlands. [7] In Susa and Ancan did they salute Innana humbly, like tiny mice. In the high mountains, the multitudes groveled in the dust for her. [8] He traversed five mountains, six mountains, seven mountains. He lifted up his eyes and saw Aratta. [9] Then did he step forth into her courtyard and make known boldly the authority of his king. [10] Openly did he speak the words of his heart, transmitting his message to the lord of Aratta.

[11] Now the Elohim yet ruled within Aratta. As ever were they proud and haughty, and they would not submit.

[12] Yet in those days, a famine was on the land, and Aratta was sore afflicted. In Shinar there was plenty, while

Aratta was in want. [13] So they struck a bargain, the two of them, that the lord of Aratta would bow his knee to Enmr-Kar should he send forth from his storehouse new barley and grain to ease the great hunger.

[14] When the messenger returned, he told Enmr-Kar of these things, and the great king agreed to abide by this agreement. [15] He measured out in full the barley from his granary, accounting also for the teeth of locusts. He loaded it on the pack-asses, and dispatched them at once to the highland kingdom. [16] With them he sent his messenger to demand recompense from the lord of Aratta, the prince of Eden.

[17] But again the Most High of Aratta would not submit. And the herald was sent back to Unuq empty-handed.

[18] For five years, for ten years Enmr-Kar waited. He bided his time as his chief steward fashioned for him a great scepter, and when it was completed, he sent it forth with his herald to the throne of Aratta.

[19] Then the lord of Aratta despaired, saying, "Aratta is indeed slaughtered like sheep. Its roads are indeed like the rebel lands, since Innana has given the kingship of Aratta over to the lord of Unuq. [20] Now Innana looks with favor on this man who has sent a herald, whose message is as clear as the light of the sun. [21] Where in Aratta can one go in this crisis? How long before the yoke we bear is tolerable? [22] As for us, in the midst of our direst hunger, most extreme famine, are we to prostrate ourselves before the lord of Unuq?"

[23] Still, he was not willing to submit.

²⁴ He therefore summoned the herald and said to him: "Say to your master, 'Let my champion compete with your champion, and let the better man prevail!' "

²⁵ Upon hearing this was Enmr-Kar enraged with his brother from the mountains. ²⁶ So told his messenger, "Accept this challenge." And he gave him other words to speak in his behalf, demanding once more gold and silver for the house of Inanna he would build in his city, and rare lapis lazuli to adorn it. ²⁷ Uttering new threats, he spoke to his messenger in an oracle at such length that the herald could not repeat all that was said. For his mouth was heavy and speech forsook him.

²⁸ Therefore did Enmr-Kar inscribe his message on a tablet of clay, as had been done in former times by Enoch. ²⁹ Until that day, the way of the scribe had long been neglected, and the practice of writing was no more established. Only the ME preserved from former times remained. ³⁰ So it was that Nimrod revived the ancient art of writing then and there, dispatching the herald with his new message engraved in clear lettering for all to see.

³¹ He brought these tablets to Aratta and presented them to the king there. And the message inscribed upon them told of what Enmr-Kar had already achieved as he built his tower up to the highest heavens: ³² "This tree has grown high, uniting the heavens with the earth. Its crown reaches up to the heaven, and its trunk is secure upon the earth. ³³ So does his kingship shine forth upon the land; it is he who sends you this clay tablet."

[34] When the lord of Aratta saw it, his brow was creased in anger. And at that very moment did the storm god unleash thunder from the heavens, and the earth shook also beneath them. [35] Like the roar of a great lion, the storm raged all about them, and the mountains convulsed beneath them, rising up in thirst to accept heaven"s offering. [35] On the parched flanks of Aratta, in the midst of the mountains, wheat sprang up of its own accord. Chickpeas grew unbidden. [36] And the men of Aratta brought these things into the granary of their lord, wherefore he looked upon them and saw that the famine had ended.

[36] Emboldened, the lord of Aratta therefore declared to the messenger: "Behold! Innana has not forsaken her people! She has neither fled from Aratta nor taken up residence in Unuq. [37] She who preserved Aratta in the midst of the flood has now blessed her anew. For as the flood swept over and we stood in the face of it, now Innana, the lady of all the lands, has seen fit to sprinkle the water of life upon her children."

Yet he knew not that in the rain she wept for them; that the waters were as tears shed for the strife he had created.

9

[1] So the lord of Aratta defied Enmr-Kar once more, and he called to him a champion who came wrapped in lion skins with a turban of many colors around his head. [2] This

man was a sorcerer, and boasted, "I shall make Unuq dig canals! I shall make them submit to the shrine of Aratta! ³ The lands from below shall submit to the lands from above, from the sea to the cedar mountain. Let Unuq bring its goods by boat in tribute in a flotilla to the great city of Aratta!"

⁴ So the lord of Aratta gave him silver and gold, promising him fine food and sweet wine should he succeed in his purpose. ⁵ "When their men are taken captive," he vowed, "your life shall be full, and you shall enjoy every happiness; in your hand shall be wealth and prosperity."

⁵ And the sorcerer directed his steps toward Unuq.

⁶ When he arrived, he cursed the livestock, so that no milk came from the udder of cow or she-goat. The kid went hungry and the cow grew bitter toward her calf. ⁷ The churn lay empty, and the day was given to starvation. ⁸ The cow-herd dropped the staff from his hand in amazement, while the shepherd hung the crook at his side and wept bitterly. ⁹ They sat down amidst the debris of their ruin and cried out, saying, "The sorcerer of Aratta has invaded the stables; he has made the milk scarce so young calves are wanting. He has made butter scarce and diminished the milk of the she-goat. So have we been dealt a disaster!"

¹⁰ And their voices were heard across creation, and reached the ears of a witch named Sajburu.

¹¹ Hearing of their plight did she turn her face toward Unuq and make her way down the Euphrates, continuing until at last she came to the great city which the sorcerer afflicted. ¹² And she challenged him, saying, "I am the

champion of Unuq. Let us have a contest, to see whose magic is from heaven, and let the loser declare on his honor that his country shall submit to the one whose magic shall triumph."

[13] To this was he agreeable.

[14] So both of them took a fish and threw it into the river. And in place of the sorcerer's fish, a giant carp arose from the waters. [15] But in place of the witch's fish, an eagle emerged and seized the carp between its talons. Then did it ascend out of the waves and away into the heavens.

[15] A second time they threw a fish into the river. And the sorcerer caused a ewe and its lamb to rise up from the waters, but the witch made a wolf come forth and lay hold of them, dragging them into the desert.

[16] A third time they threw a fish into the river. The sorcerer made a cow and its calf arise from the waters, but the witch called forth a lion to drag them away into the reedbeds.

[17] A fourth time still they threw a fish into the river, the mighty Euphrates. The sorcerer brought forth an ibex and wild sheep, but the witch summoned to her a mountain leopard that laid hold of it.

[18] A fifth time yet the sorcerer threw a fish into the water, and a gazelle kid came up from out of its current. [19] And the witch likewise threw a fish into the river, where it was transformed into a tiger that sprang up and captured the gazelle.

[20] And the sorcerer's countenance darkened, and his mind became confused. [21] He begged that she show him

mercy, but she refused, saying, "You have caused great distress in the stable and the cow shed. ²² You have removed the lunch table; barren are the tables of the morning and the evening. ²³ You have cut off butter and milk from the evening meal of the great dining hall. Such wickedness is deserving of death under the law, and I shall not pardon your life."

²⁴ Therefore did she lay hold of him and cast him headlong into the river, whereupon his life force departed from him and Aratta was finally vanquished.

²⁵ Then did Enmr-Kar send forth a mighty army against Aratta, ascending the highlands through the seven mountain passes that are the seven gates of heaven. ²⁶ There did he lay siege to the city whence his ancestors had come. His men made their encampment in the ditches and posts that surrounded the city. ²⁷ But for a year did javelins fly down at them from atop the city walls, and slingstones like raindrops fell as if from the clouds above them to the roadway where they stood. ²⁸ Around about they were hemmed in by briars and dragons, so that they despaired of ever taking the city.

²⁹ But Lugalbanda, the great general, instructed Enmr-Kar as to how he might vanquish Aratta.

³⁰ Cut down the lone tamarisk tree
By the banks of the water meadows!
Tear out the reeds that grow in that place!
³¹ Catch the fish that swims there and cook it!
So shall the waters be fouled, which are life to Aratta!

[32] Then carry off the metalworkers
and stonemasons of the city
[33] Renew it once more and settle it
Then it shall be his!

[35] So Enmr-Kar did as he was bidden. He cut down the tamarisk tree which grew alone by the banks of the water meadows, and he uprooted the reeds from that place. [36] He caught the fish from the river and cooked it, so his armies renewed their strength. [37] From the tree's wood he made himself buckets, so that water was diverted from Aratta. [38] Those within the city thirsted, but they could not drink. They hungered, but they could not eat.

[39] They opened their gates to Enmr-Kar, who took away the metalworkers and made slaves of the masons. [40] The proud Elohim of Aratta were made humble. The Most High of their number was laid low and cast down from the Kingdom of Heaven, just as the mountain lord and his minions had cast down Seth and the sons of Adam. [41] And they who had served him became as wanderers upon the earth, seeking a new home for themselves in the southern reaches of the lowlands.

[42] From that day forward did Unuq claim dominion over Eden, and the great kingdom that had been the cradle of Adam become no more than memory. [43] Ever more the vassal, it passed from one king to another, until the garden was uprooted by the feet of many armies and the wide plain was subdued beneath long caravans and new cities.

[44] But no man forgot her glory. And still, few dared defy the name of the Most High.

10

[1] Enmr-Kar built his tower to the heavens and adorned it with all manner of precious stones and metals from Aratta. [2] His armies crossed the plains and mountains, subduing the lands around him, and he laid waste all who came against him. [3] With each new conquest, his pride was magnified and with each new victory his arrogance increased. [4] In a vision he conceived of a kingdom which would span the breadth of creation, wherein the great god of Unuq would reign from horizon to horizon and he, Enmr-Kar, would rule the entire world as his very embodiment. The Enki, lord of all the earth.

[5] During his conflict with Aratta, he had sent his messenger forth with the following oracle:

[6] On the day when there is no snake
On the day when there is no scorpion
On the day when there is no hyena
[7] When there is neither lion, dog nor wolf
When there is no fear nor trembling
When man shall have no rival

[8] At this time, may the lands of Shubur and Hamazi,
The many-tongued

And Shinar, the mountain of the ME of magnificence
And Akkad, which possesses all that is fitting
And Martu, which rests in security
May the whole universe, the well-guarded people
All address the lord of the air together in a single
language

[9] At that time shall all the ambitious lords
And all the ambitious kings
And all the ambitious princes
Submit to the wise lord Enki

[10] The lord of abundance and steadfast decisions,
Known for his wisdom, the lord of Eridu
Shall change the tongues within their mouths
As many as he placed there
So the speech of mankind is truly one.

[11] Yet it was not to be.
[12] For the sorcerer of Aratta had placed a curse upon
him. And the gods did listen, because he had acted so in
violence. [13] His offense against Aratta was not to be
forgiven, for he had trampled the garden of Osiris and had
vanquished the land of Eden. He had cut down the
tamarisk tree, where Osiris had been preserved. [14] So the
gods took vengeance upon him and turned the oracle
against him. Within his empire there arose conflicts and
disputes, and these multiplied with each new phase of the

moon. [15] Many men sought to ascend the great tower he had built, but each prevented his neighbor from so doing.

[16] In the midst of their arguing, a single tongue became many. The people of Shinar were dispersed across the land while the tower was torn asunder by ruin and folly.

[17] No man understood his neighbor, for they had forgotten how to listen. The names of ancient cities were changed, so that they were no longer recognized. [18] Unuq became Uruk, and men also called it Erech. [19] Likewise the names gods and heroes from the first times were corrupted, with each tribe calling them by different appellations.

[20] Isis was Inanna and Diana and Astarte.

[21] A'bel became Ba'al, and also Bile, and Adam was Adapa.

[22] Osiris was a new name for the one once called Asar.

[23] Even the name of Enoch was dispersed upon the winds, so he was known as Thoth to the Egyptians, and Hermes to the Greeks. [24] In Akkad he was called Ea, and in the west he was Yah the Righteous, who lays his bow upon the heavens at the passing of each storm.

[25] And it came to pass that the men of each nation blessed one name and cursed another, as though the names themselves were a source of power. [26] "This name alone is holy!" they declared, condemning the use of any other. [27] On pain of death did men oppose these sacred names. And in these names were the seeds of untold violence sown to generations of widows and beggars and orphans that would follow.

[28] And the men who spoke these names defiled the sanctity of the land.

[29] They appointed priests to guard their altars, to speak in the name of their god.

[30] They appointed kings to guard their treasures, to rule in the name of their god.

[31] They appointed warriors and armies, to fight in the name of their god.

[32] And the priests hid the face of their god behind a mask, saying, "No man may see the face of a god and live!"

[33] And the masks they fashioned to hide the sacred they made in their own image, saying, "Our god is jealous," when it was they who became jealous; and "Our god demands vengeance," when the demand was their own. [34] They proclaimed, "Our god is angry" to justify their anger, and "Our god commands it!" to support their bloodshed.

11

[1] In the course of time, it came to pass that one named Lugalbanda rose up and took the throne of Unuq. [2] There were wars and rumors of wars across the land. Treaties were made and broken, and alliances were sundered. [3] Lies were the currency of commerce, and no man valued the life of his neighbor. [4] Even firstborn sons were set on the altar and butchered for the sake of their gods. [5] Yet still every tribe recalled the days of Noah. And though they called

him by different names, the story of his time was preserved in their memory, and it remains so to this day. ⁶ They took courage in his example and sought solace in his wisdom.

⁷ As this wisdom had preserved him, so they would seek it.

⁸ As his great ark had guarded him, so they would guard themselves.

⁹ As he had set forth upon the waters, so would they too venture forth.

¹⁰ Nevermore would the waters of the floodplain overwhelm them, but would bear them aloft to a land far distant. ¹¹ They would build great vessels as their father had before them, and they would turn the power of waters to fit their purpose. ¹² Rising up, the great Euphrates would bear them forward to Dilmun and beyond. Through the place of the two waters, sweet and bitter, would they pass, out across the open sea that some call Ocean.

¹³ This was the time of going forth, when mariners claimed new lands in the name of their masters. ¹⁴ The men of Kish made their way along the coastlands of the desert, never venturing far from shore as they passed beyond the realm of Sheba to the south and on to the land which is on two sides of the water. ¹⁵ On one side they came ashore and built a port which they named Aeden, after the garden of their fathers. ¹⁶ Here they buried the bones of their ancestors, Cain and A'bel. And they named the land across the channel Cush, after the city whence they had come.

¹⁷ Others, though, called it the land of Punt and those who dwelt there the Punic tribe.

[18] These were the people of the Phoenix who came from the land of the rising sun, the followers of Horus from beyond the horizon. [19] For this reason they came to be called the Phoenicians. [20] Many wild animals roamed in their kingdom, from the elephant to the hippopotamus to the baboon and leopard. [21] Their land was rich also in myrrh and incense, in ebony and short-horned cattle, and they brought into their kingdom goods from other lands around about: gold and ivory and animal skins. And they prospered there.

[22] It was they who created the first true system of letters, in the tradition of Enoch, setting them down upon scrolls of papyrus and gathering them together in libraries. [23] Indeed, the great port city of Byblos, which they founded, took its name from the inner bark of the papyrus plant.

[24] It was but one of many trading posts they established. Some took their great boats with them across the desert, finding their way at last to the Nile and making a kingdom for themselves along the banks of the great river. [25] These were the fathers of Egypt, who founded great dynasties and gave rise to a mighty empire. [26] Yet always they remembered Punt as the land of the gods, whence their ancestors had come, and traded with her rulers to the advantage of both lands.

[27] The queen of Egypt brought shiploads of goods across from Aeden to her country, loading her ships heavily with marvels from the land of Punt: all goodly fragrant woods from the gods' land, heaps of myrrh-resin with fresh

myrrh trees. [28] There was pure ivory and ebony, cinnamon wood, green gold of Amu, khesyt wood, ahmut and senter incenses, and cosmetics for the eyes. [29] Also on board were monkeys and apes, dogs and the skins of the southern panther, all brought forth by the Phoenicians and their children. [30] Never had the like of this been sent to any king enthroned since the beginning.

[31] In the image of the towers in Shinar, the kings of Egypt raised up the pyramids. And the Phoenicians built ships even greater than those that had borne them to Cush and Aeden, seeking out new lands to extend their wealth.

[32] They built Tyre on the coast of Lebanon.

[33] They built Carthage in the north of Libya.

[34] And they traveled onward to the gates of the Sea at the Center of the World, where they built Tangier on the southern land Cadiz in the north. [35] Thence they ventured farther still, driven by strong winds away from the coast of the known world. [36] They challenged the dragons that guard the ends of the earth and monsters that plied the depths of the great ocean. Yet their courage failed them not, and the pressed on until they came to a land both vast and bounteous. [37] Here they found a level plain of exceeding beauty, with mountains rising high above it, from which flowed navigable rivers that were used for irrigation.

[38] Gardens in great multitudes were traversed by streams of sweet water. Its inhabitants had built for themselves private dwellings and great halls for banquet feasts, with fields of flowers arrayed around about. [39] In the highlands were dense thickets and fruit trees of every variety, among

which could be found secluded valleys and springs of fresh, clean water.

[40] All manner of beast and wild animal did dwell there, in a land where the climes were mild and forgiving.

[41] This place became a secret and a legend, undiscovered for its distance from the known lands, until the Phoenicians landed their ships there. [42] Some among them proposed to establish a colony on those shores, but the men of Carthage sought to prevent it, fearing their own city might be forsaken because of the excellence of this new land, farther even from their homeland than was Shinar from Libya.

[43] Yet however far they traveled from their homeland, the people of the Phoenix remembered always the sacred land of Aratta, and they mourned their departure from their abode in the highlands. [44] So they built for themselves new mountains in the midst of their cities, by which they could ascend to the heavens. [45] And they fashioned for themselves arks to set at their summit, wherein they placed the tablets of truth they had inherited from their father Enoch.

12

[1] Years passed, and the tablets were forgotten, guarded by priests who neither knew their wisdom nor shared it with those who sought it.

[2] When they had locked their wisdom away, they locked themselves away as well, taking refuge behind walls and

battlements thicker and higher than any built before.
² Proud Gilgamesh took the throne of Unuq and raised the walls so high he boasted that no man could breach them. He was the son of Lugalbanda, hailed as one part man and two parts god.

³ It was in his day that the power of Kish was broken, for its lord Agga sent an army to besiege Unuq. Yet the city's wall held firm, and the assault on its ramparts failed. ⁴ So it was that Unuq reigned supreme in the land between the rivers. ⁵ But Gilgamesh's pride restrained him from true greatness, so Osiris sent a man from the mountains to test him, a man with strength and power to equal the great king's. ⁶ This one was called Enkidu, and he came out of the highlands like a terror, his body covered in hair and his mane long and flowing.

⁷ He went forth like a prowling lion, eating with the gazelles and drinking with the beasts. He struck fear into the hearts of all who saw him. ⁸ So it was that when a certain hunter came upon him at the watering hole, this man was astonished, and retreated at once to his own home. ⁹ Thence he went to Unuq, and reported to Gilgamesh the marvel that he had seen.

¹⁰ "I saw a young man come down from the mountain, strong and powerful as a sky bolt from heaven. His feet tread upon the mountains and he eats among the cattle. ¹¹ When he comes to the watering place, I dare not approach him. When I dig a pit, he fills it. When I set a trap, he destroys it. ¹² Because of him, the beasts of the

field elude me, so that I can no longer make my living there."

[13] So Gilgamesh called to him the wise woman Shamhat and sent her with the hunter, and he told the man what he must do. And they went their way.

[14] At length they came to the watering hole, and they waited there for Enkidu. [15] When at length he came to that place, the hunter said to his companion, "Shamhat, shrink not from him when he approaches, but let him know the ways of a woman. Then will he forget the beasts of the open field, and will lavish his attentions upon you!"

[16] And it came to pass as he had said, and Enkidu abode with the wise woman for six days and seven nights. [17] And when the time was completed, behold, no longer did the beasts of the field approach him, but were wary and kept their distance. [18] His strength had been diminished, but yet had he acquired judgment. The woman's gift to him was wisdom. [19] Gazing hard upon his face, she spoke thus to him:

"You have grown wise now, Enkidu, like unto a god. Why should you roam the open country with the beasts? [20] Come and let me show you the sheepfold of Unuq, where Gilgamesh rules in perfect power like a wild bull, stronger yet than all the people."

[21] And she divided her garments between them, so he could clothe himself, and she took him to the tents of the shepherds. [22] There did the shepherds gather round and look upon him in amazement. Surely this was not the same one who had roamed about the open lands so freely?

²³ Quickly did they bring him bread and strong wine, yet he knew not how to partake, for he had but suckled the milk of wild creatures. ²⁴ Yet the woman came to him and showed him, saying, "Take of the bread, the staff of life, and drink of the wine, for it is custom."

²⁵ For this was the mystery of the bread and the cup, the first for life and the second for knowledge.

²⁶ And he did as she had bidden. He partook of the fruit that came from the vine, the nectar of knowledge for good and for ill. ²⁷ And he broke bread, which was the food of Osiris, in the hope of eternal life. Yet eternal life would not be his.

²⁸ Then did the mighty Enkidu array himself in the clothing of men, so that he took on the aspect of a bridegroom. ²⁹ And when he did so, the shepherds cheered him, and he exulted in the spirit that the wine bestowed upon him. ³⁰ And he became a watchman for the sheepfold, hunting lions and wolves that stalked them while the shepherds took their rest. ³¹ He was a mighty guardian, and in strength he knew no rival.

³² Thus did the days pass, good and many.

³³ Then at length did a weary traveler come upon them from the land of Unuq. And Enkidu welcomed the stranger into his presence.

³⁴ "What news? And wherefore have you come?" he asked him.

³⁵ And the man replied, saying, "Gilgamesh has gone into the marriage house and shuts out the people. He does strange things in Unuq, the city of great streets. ³⁶ He

commands work at the roll of the drum for men and women, and he demands that he be first to share a new bride's marriage bed, before even her husband can know her. [37] For he says this is his birthright, ordained by the gods themselves in the heavens. Even now does he prepare to enter into the bridal chamber!"

[38] Therefore did Enkidu grow pale with anger. And he clenched his fists, declaring boldly, "Now I will go to this place where Gilgamesh afflicts the people! [39] Now will I challenge him to his face, and will proclaim aloud in Unuq, 'I have come to abolish the old order, for in strength no man can surpass me!'"

[40] So he strode forth with the wise woman until he came to the great city of Unuq. [41] And he made his way into the great marketplace, parting the crowds as they exclaimed of him, "This is the man who was raised with the beasts. Behold! He is a match even for the great Gilgamesh!"

[42] And as Gilgamesh made ready to enter the bridal chamber, Enkidu stepped forth and stood before him, barring the way so he could not pass. [43] Gilgamesh sought to move forward, yet he put out his foot and so prevented it. [44] Then did the two men fall upon one another, grappling and snorting like two great bulls. The walls shook and the doorposts trembled until they shattered, unable to bear the strength of the two great warriors.

[45] At last did Gilgamesh bend his knee and plant his foot in the earth, and he turned his body so Enkidu was thrown. [46] Thus was the great contest between them ended, and Enkidu said to the man who had bested him, "There is no

one like you in all the earth. Your strength surpasses the strength of all men." [47] In that same moment, the two men were bonded, and from that time forward, they were constant friends.

[48] But the gods did not forget Gilgamesh's hubris, nor did they ignore the grave offense he had shown in taking other men's wives to his own bed. [49] And they said to themselves, "Behold, here is one who might have been worthy to be called immortal. Yet now he is cursed to know not only his own greatness, yet also the certainty of his death."

13

[1] Such was the fame of Gilgamesh and Enkidu that great tales of their exploits are told to this very day. Are they not to be found in the "Book of Gilgamesh and Enkidu" and "The Bull of Heaven"?

[2] There is it written that the two warriors fought the bull of heaven, and that Enkidu seized it by the horns while Gilgamesh slew it with a single thrust of his sword. [3] Its heart they offered to the sun, and its horns they took with them to adorn the walls of Gilgamesh's palace in Unuq. [4] But Inanna was enraged at their actions and took her case before the council of the gods. Therefore was it decided that, in exchange for the bull's life, one of the two heroes would forfeit his own.

[5] It was decreed that Enkidu should be the one to die, and though Gilgamesh lamented long over his stricken

friend, there was naught he could do to spare him from the fate that awaited him. [6] One day passed, and Enkidu lay still, taken by fever. A second day passed, and his sickness increased. A third day, and he grew weaker, his eyes blinded by tears from weeping. [7] And after twelve days, he called out to Gilgamesh, saying, "My friend, the great goddess has cursed me to die in shame. I shall not die like a warrior in battle. I feared that end, yet happy is the man who dies in combat, for I must die in shame."

[8] And at length he breathed his last, leaving his companion to weep bitter tears at his passing. Gilgamesh touched his heart, yet it beat no more. [9] So he laid a veil across Enkidu, as one puts a veil across the countenance of a bride. Such was his affection for his fallen friend.

[10] Then did Gilgamesh rage about like a lioness whose cubs are taken from her, and he flung his royal garments from him as if they were abominations. [11] He declared, in his grief, "All the people of Unuq shall weep over you, and they shall raise a dirge of the dead. The joyful shall bend low in sorrow, and I will grow my hair long in tribute to your greatness! [12] Then shall I wander the desert places, adorned in nothing more than the skin of a lion!"

[13] And so it came to pass that he departed the gates of Unuq, knowing not where he would go, yet fearful in his heart that he should suffer the same fate as his companion. [14] "How can I rest?" he asked himself. "How can I know peace? My heart is stricken with despair. What has become of my brother shall likewise befall me at the end of my days."

¹⁵ So he determined in his heart to find his ancestor Noah, of whom it was said he had never perished, for he had found favor with the gods. ¹⁶ He traveled a great distance until he came to the waters of death, across which lay the land of the rising sun. This, he had been told, was the land of Noah. ¹⁷ And on the shore was a ferryman, a servant of Noah, who stood ready to bear him across the waters.

¹⁸ When he arrived at the habitation of Noah, he asked the ancient one to share with him the secret of life eternal.

¹⁹ This, then, is what Noah told him: "There is a plant that grows under the water, thorny like a rose. It will wound your hands when you try to lay hold of it, yet if you succeed in so doing, you will hold in your hands that which restores lost youth to a man!"

²⁰ Gilgamesh therefore found the deepest channel in the open waters and tied heavy stones to each of his feet, that he might descend into the depths of the ocean. ²¹ There he found the plant of which Noah had spoken, and he plucked it from the place it was growing. ²² Its thorns pierced his hands, but he held it fast. Then he cut the stones from the chords by which they were fastened to his feet, and the water's current took him until he was safe upon the shore.

²³ Gilgamesh, triumphant, boasted of what he had accomplished. He exulted to the ferryman, saying, "Come and see this marvelous plant, by virtue of which a man may regain his former strength! ²⁴ I shall bear it forth to Unuq of the strong walls, and once there, I shall give it to all the

elders of the people to eat. [25] Its name shall be 'Old Men are Young Once More,' and at the last I shall partake of it myself, that my lost youth may be restored."

[26] Then did they go on their way, and at length did they stop for the evening at pond of cool water. And laying the plant aside, Gilgamesh went down to the water to bathe. [27] Yet deep within the pool there lay a serpent, and it sensed the sweetness of the flower. So it rose up from out of the water and snatched it away before Gilgamesh could reach the place where he had lain it. And he knew he could not recover it.

[28] At the end of his appointed days, therefore, Gilgamesh breathed his last. And a dirge was sung for him when Unuq laid him in the earth.

[29] The king has laid himself down — he will not rise again
The lord of Kullub — he will not rise again
He conquered evil — he will not come again

[30] He was strong of arm — he will not rise again
He had a countenance well-pleasing —
    he will not come again
He is gone into the mountain —
    he will not come again

[31] On the bed of fate he lies — he will not rise again
From the couch of many colors, he will not rise again

The Book of

Pharaohs

1

[1] Hearken now to the Book of the Pharaohs, who ruled the land called Egypt by the Nile. These rose up to challenge Babylon, to become its equal and surpass it. [2] They raised up monuments in the desert and sought their counsel among the stars. These were the people of Osiris, the servants of the sun.

³ In Babylon, the kingdom of Gilgamesh was weakened, and a new city rose to claim the mantle of greatness. This was Akkad, which Enmr-Kar had ruled in earlier times. ⁴ Yet now a king arose there even greater than he, whose empire stretched from Elam to the cedars of Lebanon.

⁵ In Kish did he rise to power, emboldened by a dream in which he saw the king there meet his death by drowning. ⁶ He said, "I am the Gardener!" after the manner of Osiris. And "Isis is my consort!" that he might claim the mantle of wisdom. But he called her Ishtar, after the manner of his people.

⁷ "My mother was high priestess, yet my father I knew not," he declared. ⁸ "My city is Azupiranu, on the banks of the great Euphrates. There did my mother conceive me; in secret did she bear me. ⁹ She set me in an ark of rushes, sealing the lid tight shut with bitumen. Then did she cast me into the river, which rose quickly. And it bore me on its waters to the home of Akki, the water drawer. ¹⁰ Then he became as a father to me, raising me up to be his gardener. And Ishtar did love me, and did grant to me the kingship."

¹¹ Sargon was from the tribe of the Shemites, and he was the first among his people to rule in the land of Shinar. ¹² His tongue was foreign to them, but his armies swept across the land like locusts, and none could stand against him. ¹³ Lugalzaggesi of Unuq had bound all of Shinar to him as a single land. Yet he fell to the Akkadian like a sandman shaking his fist in defiance at the sea god Yam.

¹⁴ Sargon tore down the battlements of Unuq and brought Lugalzaggesi in a dog collar to the gates of Enlil.

¹⁵ Then did he march forth against Ur and Lagash, and thence to the shores of the southern sea, where he cleansed his weapons of all enemy blood and proclaimed himself master of all that met his gaze.

¹⁶ He had no rival, and no man was his equal. His splendor covered all the lands, and by the eleventh year of his reign he had subdued the lands in the west to their most distant shoreline. ¹⁷ In his pride did he set up statues to his glory, and took from the far lands tribute, which he ferried on barges to his palace in Akkad. ¹⁸ And when the land of Kazallu defied him, he laid it waste so that not a single perch was left for the birds of the heavens.

¹⁹ Mari he subdued, and Ebla did submit to him. He made himself Susa's master and traded with the cities of India, Crete and Cappadocia.

²⁰ And the Shemites prospered in the land between the rivers, and their numbers multiplied while Sargon and his scions reigned there. ²¹ For fifty-six years did he hold the seat of power, and after him his children, and their children after them. ²² But Naram-Sin, the grandson of Sargon, stretched forth his hand against the city of Nippur, and he defiled the temple of Enlil in that place. ²³ Therefore did the gods grow wroth with his insolence and withdraw their favor from Akkad.

²⁴ For the first time since the foundation of their cities, the great fields yielded no grain. The fisheries yielded no fish. The orchards produced neither wine nor syrup. ²⁵ Clouds gathered but withheld their rain, and the masgurum tree grew not. ²⁶ In that day, a shekel's worth of

oil was but half a quart, and a shekel's worth of grain was but half a quart. Such were the prices in the markets of every city. ²⁷ He who slept on the roof died on the roof. He who slept in the house had no burial. And the people scourged themselves in the anguish of their hunger.

²⁸ So did the empire of Sargon fall. And in its place rose a new line of rulers who restored the name of Shinar to its former place. ²⁹ The sons of Shem were cast down from their places of privilege, and their language was stricken from the books of the law. And those who were of royal heritage feared for their safety, that they might be set upon and slain by men who hated them. ³⁰ So it was with one named Terach, who dwelt in the precincts of Ur during those days. And he had three sons there with him, whose names were Abram, Nahor and Haran.

³¹ Abram was the eldest among him and heir to the lineage of Terach, for his name meant "exalted father." ³² He married a woman of Shemite noble lineage, for her name was Sarai, which translated means, "my princess." ³³ Haran, in like manner, was of noble heritage, for his eldest daughter he named Milcah, which means "queen." He was also the father of Lot. ³⁴ Yet he departed this earth while his father yet lived, and Milcah married his brother, Nahor, that he might care for her.

³⁵ Now it came to pass that Milcah was with child by Nahor, and she gave birth to eight sons, the youngest of whom she called Bethuel. And Bethuel begat a son named Laban and a daughter named Rebekah.

2

¹ Upon the death of Haran, a dispute arose concerning Terach's inheritance. Although Abram was the eldest, his wife was barren and had given him no child to preserve their lineage. ² Haran's son Lot therefore sought the inheritance, and this was a cause of strife between them, for Abram said, "Sarai may yet conceive." But Lot said, "She is past the age of childbirth, and the birthright shall pass to me."

³ News of their dispute was heard upon the streets of Ur, and it reached the ears of the king in Shinar. ⁴ He feared lest the clan of Terach raise an army to fight against them, whereupon he sought to quench the fire of rebellion ere it was kindled. ⁵ He therefore set forth a decree that the clan of Terach be exiled from the city of Ur and from the entire land of Shinar, so Terach took his kinsmen and fled that place for Harran, a city of Ebla to the north and to the west. ⁶ There did they settle, in Paddan Aram (which means "the highland plain"), until the death of Terach.

⁷ But there was famine upon the land, and the people of Harran were loath to share their pastures with the sons of Terach. ⁸ Then there arose a dispute within the clan of Terach, for some proposed that they should leave that place while others among them wished to tarry there. ⁹ So it was that Nahor and his family remained upon the highland plain, with his son Bethuel and his kinfolk Laban and

Rebekah. But Abram and his kinsmen departed that place and went down into Canaan, and thence into the land of Egypt, by the banks of the fertile Nile. [10] Lot and his wife accompanied them. [11] Their numbers had swollen, both in men and among their livestock, and their servants were as an army of invaders in lower Egypt. To the Egyptians, they were the Hyksos or the "foreigners," and others called them the Habiru.

[12] Now the pharaoh in that day was weak, and feared the numbers in the Hyksos caravan, so he sought an alliance with Abram as a means to secure the throne of his kingdom. [13] When he saw Sarai among their number, that she was comely and pleasing in her manner, he sought her hand as a way to seal their friendship. For Abram had said to him, "She is my sister." [14] And knowing not that they were married, the pharaoh became set on having her. [15] To this end did he invite her to the palace, and in return for her attentions did he give Abram a wealth of sheep and cattle, with donkeys and camels for his herdsmen, and servants male and female.

[16] But his household became afflicted with disease and pestilence, and he grew fearful when his ministers said to him, "Your betrothed is wed already, and Abram is her master."

[17] So he summoned Abram to him and said to him, "What is this that you have done to me? Why did you withheld from me the knowledge that she is your wife?"

[18] And Abram had no answer for him. Yea, he had kept this a secret knowingly, for he sought to enrich himself

with gifts from Egypt, that he might enhance his own might at the pharaoh's expense. [19] And this much did he indeed accomplish, for the pharaoh pleaded with him to go his way, saying of Sarai, "Take her and go!" [20] And the king instructed his servants to send Abram on his way, along with his wife and everything he had — the herds he had arrived with and the gifts he had been given from the pharaoh's own wealth.

[21] So it was that Abram's power greatly increased, and the pharaoh's hand was weakened. [22] Therefore did the pharaoh withdraw to his capital in the south, leaving to Abram and his people the marshes and lowlands near the mouth of the mighty Nile. These lands became a kingdom to him, and he prospered in all his endeavors. [23] To the Egyptians, he was Maibre Sheshy, pharaoh of the lower kingdom, and his lands extended into the desert south of Canaan. [24] He amassed great quantities of gold and of silver, and the pharaoh of old became his servant, and he ascended the throne of Egypt.

[25] In the course of time, he went forth, up out of Egypt into the Negev, and thence to a place called Bethel. But the quarreling between Abram and his nephew Lot was resumed, for Lot had grown jealous of Abram's wealth and Sarai still had borne him no issue. [26] Abram therefore called his nephew to him, saying, "Let there be no more quarrels between the two of us, or between your herders and my own. [27] Is not the whole land spread forth in front of you? Therefore, let the two of us part company on this day. If you take the path to the left-hand side, I shall continue on

the right. And if you choose the right-hand path, I shall follow the left." [28] For he knew that his armies were the stronger among the two of them, and that the lowlands of the Nile had sworn allegiance to his lordship.

[29] Therefore Lot surveyed the land before them and, seeing the verdant plain of the Jordan to the east of them, chose this path for his men and his livestock. [30] He came upon the city of Sodom and abode there, in lowlands so rich with pasture that they recalled the land of Eden. This was the Vale of Siddim, which means "valley of broad plains."

[31] But Abram took his retinue to the west and settled there in the land of Canaan. And the Elohim dwelt there in that day, as did also descendants of the sons of Adam. [32] And the Elohim mingled among the men who were with them, and they went in among the daughters of Adam and knew them, for they saw that they were comely and delightful to the flesh.

[33] And they built themselves a city and called it Salem, and this became for them a new Eden, forged on a hilltop in the midst of Canaan. There did they reconvene the council of the Elohim, and choose one among themselves to bear the title of Most High, as in days of old. [34] A priest was chosen among them as the leader of the Malachim, who would serve as messenger to the country around about there. [35] The name of this one was Melchizedek.

Like Abram, he was a Shemite.

3

[1] Now when Lot had settled in Sodom, he did not seek to make himself king there, for that place was in thrall to Chederlaomer the king of Elam. [2] In those days the Elamites had marched westward out of Susa, gathering to themselves the lands between the rivers in Shinar where Sargon had once held sway. [3] Two kings from this place did they count among their servants, and likewise the ruler of the Hittites to the north. [4] With the armies of these cities at his side, Chederlaomer had swept down to claim all the lands to the east of Canaan as his own, and none dared oppose him.

[5] When Lot arrived in Sodom, he likewise fell under the sway of Chederlaomer, who was the enemy of Abram. [6] But when the five kings of Siddim learned of his presence, they said to himself, "Who is this among us now? Is it not the nephew of Egypt's pharaoh? And shall he not protect us from the wrath of the Elamites?" [7] They did not know that Abram and Lot had parted ways, and that the two were yet at enmity over the inheritance of Terach. They knew only that they could never oppose Chederlaomer alone. [8] Yet if Egypt could be persuaded to send its army to fight alongside them, then they might free themselves of the shackles that had bound them to Elam these twelve years.

[9] Therefore did the kings of Siddim refuse to send the tribute demanded by Elam, and did defy Chederlaomer.

[10] Being enraged at this, the king assembled the armies of the Hittites and of Shinar and of Larsa, along with his own, and marched forth to meet the five kings who had dared to rise up against him. They were as follows:

[11] The king of Gomorrah, which means "submerged," for it lay low in the plain and the waters would assail it when the floods came. Therefore was it well watered.

[12] The king of Admah, which means "earthen," for it was on higher ground and surrounded by earthen ramparts.

[13] The city of Bela, also called Zoar, which means "small," for it was the smallest of the five cities.

[14] The city of Zohim, which means "place of the gazelle," for deer and other animals could be seen around about there.

[15] The city of Sodom, which means "burning," as it was lacking in shade and the rays of the sun beat down upon it so fiercely that its people could find no refuge in the heat of summer. Yet this was the greatest of the cities.

[16] Though they gathered together, the armies of the five kings who assembled could not hope to match the strength of the Elamite minions, even as these had come a great distance to do battle. [17] It therefore came to pass that the Elamites and their allies fell upon them with great fury, and the kings of Sodom and Gomorrah fled before them, their armies retreating in such confusion that many among their number fell into the tar pits that were there in the valley. [18] And Abram's armies did not come forth, as they had hoped, to join their numbers. So it happened that all their

goods and food were plundered, to be taken away as the spoils of war to Elam.

20 Lot was taken captive also, along with his possessions, for the Elamites knew well who he was. And they said to themselves, "Behold, we have captured the nephew of the king of Egypt! He shall bring a great ransom, and his uncle shall bow the knee to Chederlaomer!"

21 When news was brought to Abram of what had happened, he took counsel with his advisors as to what he should do. 22 On the one hand, he reasoned, he could allow the Elamites to go their way and rid him of his nephew. Then could he claim at last Terach's inheritance. 23 Yet this matter had become to him as a flea on the back of a donkey. 24 Was Abram not now the ruler of Lower Egypt? And was not his wealth many times that of his father's treasure? 25 No, it availed him little to let the Elamites have their way, and were he to do so, he knew that his name would mocked in the camp of his enemies. 26 Then might Elam beset him from the north, or the king of Upper Egypt from the south.

27 The appearance of such weakness he could in no wise allow, so he set out with more than three hundred mercenaries and pursued the enemy. 28 He fell upon them to the north of Damascus, dividing his men up to attack from this and that way. 29 There he routed the armies of the Elamites and set them on their heels, recovering all that they had taken from the five kings and increasing his own wealth accordingly.

³⁰ Lot's wealth he did also recover, ensuring that his nephew would remain indebted to him from that day forward. In this way was the matter of Terach's inheritance laid to rest at last between them, for Lot knew that he dared not broach the matter again in the face of his uncle's power.

³¹ Therefore did Abram pledge his inheritance to Eliezer of Damascus, a servant who had followed him faithfully into battle against the Elamites.

³² After these things, they marched back down to Canaan.

4

¹ When the Elohim heard news of Abram's success, they saw the chance to magnify themselves as in days of old. Drunk with success, Abram would be generous if they could persuade him to accept their blessing — along with the promise that they would guard his eastern flank for him in wartime. ² So they sent Melchizedek forth to meet him, bearing a feast of bread and wine as an offering of peace, for Salem's men had taken no side in the war with Elam, and they feared that the king of Egypt might hold this against them should they presume to approach him empty handed.

³ Abram therefore made a treaty with him. And he gave Melchizedek a tenth of all the spoils, that he might fortify the land against Elam. ⁴ But Melchizedek said to him, "Keep the spoils, but let me have the people." (He said this

that Abram might leave a contingent behind him to help fortify the frontier against incursion.) ⁵ And Abram was pleased with this, and received the blessing of the Most High as the seal of their friendship.

⁶ The name of Salem was greatly magnified, and the power of the Elohim was strengthened by the hand of Egpyt.

⁷ Then did the king of Sodom come forth likewise to greet Abram in that place, the Valley of Shaveh, which was called the Valley of the King. ⁸ And he, too, brought an offering to appease the pharaoh, for the disgrace of his retreat had become known across the land, and he was full of dread that Abram might deal harshly with one who had yielded up his nephew into the hands of the enemy.

⁹ But when he brought forth his offering, Abram received it not, saying, "I have sworn an oath to the Most High that I will take nothing which belongs to you. ¹⁰ Not so much as a thread or a strap from one of your sandals shall I accept. For I have sworn that you shall never say, 'Abram I have enriched.' ¹¹ Nay. All that I shall have from you is what my men have eaten and the portion that belongs to those who went out with me: let the men of Aner, Eshkol and Mamre have their share."

¹² He did this because of the Sodomite king's cowardice, by which Abram knew he could not be trusted to defend the eastern outposts against Elam. ¹³ His city's defenses had been breached too easily, yet the city of Salem had been built atop a plateau amid the mountains. Thence did it offer a position of a strength from which an army might

withstand a siege or assail an enemy. [14] It was, Abram judged, a high place blessed by the gods.

[15] So Abram asked Melchizedek, "Who are the gods of this place?"

[16] Melchizedek said to him, "Our god is Enki, lord of the earth, who ruled Eden and saved Noah from the flood by the word of his mouth. And his son is the Most High, who sits upon the throne of the Elohim in Salem."

[17] And Abram said to him, "Noah was the father of my ancestor Shem, for whom the tribe of the Shemites is named. I am Abram, son of Terach. [18] My kinsmen and I fled Shinar when the days of Sargon's line were ended, for we were of noble blood and they feared our people."

[18] "Truly," said the priest of Salem, "it is Enki who has guided you to this place and delivered wealth into your hands more bountiful than that of all Shinar. The entire world now trembles before you, and the king of Elam cowers like a dog in the face of your army. [19] This oracle do I give unto you now, as in a vision, for in a vision it comes to us both here as we stand together. [20] Ea says, 'Fear not, Abram, son of Terach, for I am your shield and your greatest reward!'"

[21] Upon hearing this, Abram was sore afflicted, and he grieved at having pledged his inheritance to Eliezer of Damascus, but he had vowed also that Lot should never lay hold of it. [22] He grieved over these things before Melchizedek, saying, "Enki has given me no children, therefore shall a servant of a household be my heir."

[23] But Melchizedek shook his head and said to him, "This man shall no more be your heir than shall your ass or heifer. Nay, a son of your own loins shall succeed you." [24] He then took Abram outside, and they surveyed the heavens. "See the sky! And count the stars! Can you count them indeed, or is it beyond your power? [25] By the witness of the Watchers who sit with Enki in the heavens, as the stars are beyond numbering, so shall your offspring be! [26] For did not Enki bring you up out of Ur and make of you a mighty ruler? In this same way shall he bear your sons up, and make of them a wondrous nation!"

[27] Then Abram believed him.

[28] And Melchizedek told him, "Enki would have you find a heifer and a goat and a ram, each of which have passed three summers, and find also a dove and a young pigeon. Then bring them to me!"

[29] These things did Abram do. And he severed the bodies of each in twain, except for the birds, and arranged the segments opposite each other. [30] When, therefore, the sun had set, two servants came forth from Salem with a blazing torch and a smoking firepot to pass between the portions of each sacrifice. [31] And Melchizedek, the priest of my Salem, declared to Abram: "To your descendants shall Enki grant the lands from the river of Egypt to the great Euphrates — the lands of the Kenites and the Kenizzites, the Kadmonites and the Hittites, the Perizzites, Rephaites, Amorites, Girgasites and Jebusites, and all those who dwell in the land of Canaan."

[32] But behold, these lands already stood in thrall to Abram, for this was the true meaning of pact the priest had set before them: that one half of all the earth should belong to Egypt, and the other half should be for Salem; that all men's possessions should belong to the pharaoh, yet their lives should be pledged to Enki. [33] Henceforth should kings and priests do battle, and brother should rise against brother. [34] For one son of Abram, by his housemaid, would become the father of a people, and that another son, by Sarai, should give birth to a different nation. [35] There should ever be division between them. Isaac would ever crush the head of his brother Ishmael, yet Ishmael would strike in vengeance at his heel. [36] This was the legacy of Eden, and the wages of the enmity between Lot and Abraham. [37] The seeds of violence would they sow within their children, and their children's children after them, teaching them the way of rancor throughout a thousand generations.

[38] But it came to pass that Enki looked down upon these things and lamented what was being wrought in his name, saying, "The Elohim have taken my name in vain, and spoken without leave in my behalf. [39] They have forgotten the command of Osiris, who warned them to 'speak not in the name of any god, for such is unfettered arrogance, but let thy words redeem themselves.' [40] Therefore do I decree that no man's lips shall utter my name from this day forward. For no mere mortal should presume to speak for me!"

⁴¹ Because of this, the lips of the Elohim were sealed shut against the name of Enki. They dared not speak, nor commit it to tablet or scroll, for they feared the great god's judgment. ⁴² Instead did they speak of him as Yah, a name like unto his ancient name of Ea. ⁴³ And whenever anyone asked them by whose authority they had uttered a blessing, they would say, "I am who I am, and he is who he is." ⁴⁴ And so the saying passed from generation to generation, until its meaning was lost to the children of Salem. And they said to themselves, " 'I am' is the name of the great god whom we worship."

⁴⁵ So it was that the word for "I am" in their own tongue was taken to be the name of a god. And so was Enki's purpose confounded. ⁴⁶ Yet all these things were observed by the Watchers and inscribed in the book of the heavens, just as they had been from the beginning, to be revealed in the course of time.

⁴⁷ And these words are that revelation.

He who has ears to hear, let him hear.

5

¹ Now the gods had grown weary of the ways of men, for the sons of Adam had turned their backs on wisdom to chase after their own vanity and folly. ² So the gods withdrew from the land of Canaan and left the Shemites to worship the god they had set up upon their altars. ³ The Elohim did magnify his name and say, "The seat of heaven has been carried down to Salem."

[4] But the gods of old watched over the lands of Upper Egypt and of Babylon, of Greece and Persia, even unto the mighty Indus. [5] Their eyes were diverted to the Phoenicians and the Minoans, and to all the other peoples who had not forsaken them. The sons of Ham and the people of Japheth did revere them. [6] Many in their number withdrew westward, to the isles beyond the Sea at the Center of the World, and further still into the mists where few dared venture. [7] But they left Abram and the Shemites to worship the god he called "I am" in that place which was called Salem, where he had built a fortress atop the plateau as a bulwark for his armies. [8] He called this fortress Zion, which means "castle," and there he housed the army that would guard Egypt's eastern flank.

[9] Abram ruled over the land for ten years. But the god who was born on Zion gave him no heir, and his patience waned. [10] So it came to pass that Sarai, fearing he might put her aside for another, told him, "Sleep then with my slave girl, that she might conceive and we may build a family from her womb." [11] And Abram did as she bade him. He took Hagar to wife, as was the custom of the pharaohs (for it was their wont to take for themselves a harem full of wives). [12] He brought her to his bed, wherefore she did conceive the son for which he had longed.

[13] But Sarai was ill pleased with these events, for Hagar was a daughter of Egypt and of the southern pharaoh. [14] She had not thought that Abram would accept her offer, and when he did, she had hoped that Hagar would not conceive. [15] But now that these things had come to pass,

there could be no doubt that the people would laud this servant girl as their queen — this vassal who would deliver an heir to their beloved pharaoh.

[16] Sarai therefore said to Abram: "May the god you serve judge between the two of us. I have delivered my slave girl into your arms, and now she is raised up against me!"

[17] There was venom in her voice, and a fury born from the fires of hatred. Because of this did Hagar flee from her sight, fearing for her safety and for the life of her son. [18] She made her way down through the desert and back toward her homeland, Egypt, for she said to herself: "There shall they accept me, and my son shall be recognized as the true king once Abram has breathed his last." [19] Yet Abram knew of her intent and sent forth one of the Malachim to find her, and the messenger came upon her beside a spring in the Wilderness of Shur, near Egypt. [20] Then did he question her, saying, "Where is it you are going?"

[21] Hagar said to him, "I am fleeing from the wrath of Sarai."

[22] But the Malach said to him, "Nay, but return whence you came, and the child who is in your womb shall become the father of a race too great to count."

[23] Hearing this, Hagar knew that Abram would guard her, and that her unborn child was likewise under his protection. [24] She said to herself, "surely a god has heard me," and resolved in that moment that if her child should be a son, she would name him Ishmael, which means "the god hears." [25] Therefore it came to pass that she returned once again to Abram, and there gave birth to the child he

had fathered upon her. And behold, it was the son whom she had longed for. [26] She therefore said to herself, "My destiny is secure, for I am the mother of his only heir, and my son shall rule the earth from river to river!"

[27] And so it would have been. Yet there came a day when Sarai, too, was found to be with child, though her childbearing years were thought to have been long past her. [28] Her child, too, was a son, and she named him Isaac, which means "he laughs." This name was meant as a foreshadowing: that Isaac would laugh at the misfortunes of his half-brother and rejoice to see the son of Hagar serve him.

[29] This, truly, was Sarai's purpose and intent. And as soon as the child had been weaned, she went to Abram and laid claim to Isaac's birthright. Hatred returned to her voice, and her countenance was darkened by fury. [30] "As favorite wife of my husband the pharaoh, I demand that my son be named heir to the throne!" she told Abram. "This is my will, dear husband: Be rid of that slave woman and her cursed son at once! Never shall my son Isaac share your fortune with that bastard, Ishmael!"

[31] On hearing her, Abram was grieved and sore afraid, for he knew not what she might do to young Ishmael. [32] Yet he was determined that no harm should come to the boy, so he summoned Hagar to him and entreated her to depart from there. [33] He gave her food and water, that they might be nourished, and he ordered his men to spirit her away into the desert. And though Sarai knew it not, his men watched over them.

³⁴ When the water from her skins was wanting, he sent one among the Malachim out to console them and to bring them sustenance. ³⁵ When they cried out in distress, a messenger from Abram gave them solace in his encampment, saying, "Fear not, but lift the boy up by his hand, and he shall become a mighty nation!"

³⁶ And when she was let into one of the tents, she looked up and beheld the man before her, and she saw it was her husband. ³⁷ Still she feared him because of Sarai, and she lowered her eyes again before him, thinking that he should strike her.

³⁸ She therefore spoke to him this entreaty: "The gods are with you in all you do. Therefore swear to me that you shall not deal falsely with me or my child, or with his descendants after him. The nation of my father, mighty Egypt, showed you kindness when you were a foreigner."

³⁹ He said, "I swear it." And he took her to a spring of water welling up there in the desert, for which reason this spring is called to this day Beersheba, which means "the well of the oath."

³⁹ This was the oath he swore to her face. He swore it not to another king, as some have told it, but to the woman who gave birth to his first-born child, the one named Ishmael.

6

¹ In the course of time, Abram was troubled because he

had cast Ishmael out, and grieved because he loved the boy's mother. ² "What is this thing I have done?" he cried out to the hills. "Have I not cast out my own flesh? Have I not shunned my own true heir?" ³ And though he had acted for Ishmael's protection, the shame of it consumed him, so that it was more than he could bear.

⁴ Now a fever came upon him, and his remorse became delirium, so that he thought to atone for this thing he had done by spilling blood — the blood of Isaac. ⁵ In his head, the voice of a phantom cried out to him. At first he betook it to be the voice of Ishmael, which was shaming him. But then, as his fever was magnified, he came to hear in it the voice of Yah. ⁶ It said to him, "Take your son, your only son by Sarai, to the place that I will show you. Bind him hand and foot, as you would an animal. ⁷ Then offer him up as a sacrifice to my glory, that you may atone now for your sinfulness and the earth may know that I am God!"

⁸ So Abram cast aside his bedclothes and made haste to call his son Isaac to him, saying, "Come, and we shall make sacrifice!" ⁹ But he told not Isaac the intent of his madness, for some portion of him recalled the commandment of Osiris: "Slay neither man nor beast for gain or glory, and spill no blood on the altar of pride, for such is the way of the ingrate." ¹⁰ And he was ashamed. In his subterfuge he therefore broke another of these commandments: "Accuse no man falsely, but cast aside deception and hypocrisy." ¹¹ He justified the one for the sake of the other, because of his guilt over Ishmael, and because he thought Yah had so decreed.

[12] So he took Isaac to the top of a great mountain and bound him there to a rock, against his will. And he raised up the knife as if to cleave his flesh. [13] Yet in that moment, he hesitated. His fever lifted and the voices he had heard abated. [14] And he said to himself, "What madness is this that has consumed me? I have cast out one son at my elder wife's bidding. Will I now compound this folly by spilling the blood of his brother? Nay!"

[15] In that moment his eyes fell upon a ram caught in a thicket. "What great fortune!" he exclaimed, and stepped forward toward the place where it was tangled. [16] But he pitied not the poor trapped creature, though Osiris had forbidden such a sacrifice — whether it be of animals or of men. [17] Though his fever had broken, neither his shame nor his fury had diminished. [18] And he sought to save face for himself; his pride consumed him as he slashed at the flesh of the ram and laid its carcass on the altar he had meant for his second-born son.

[19] And the gods spoke among themselves and said, "Behold, the man has become as A'bel, shedding the blood of animals in the cause of pride and fury. [20] And he has become like Cain, for he would have shed the blood of his own kinsman just as soon. [21] Abram regards life not as a gift, but as a thing which he might take at his good pleasure. [22] Therefore shall we consign him to the fate which he has chosen. No more shall he be called Abram, which means 'exalted father,' for no more shall he be exalted. [23] Instead shall he be cast down among the nations. And he shall be called Abraham, which means 'the father

of a multitude,' for though he would have shed the blood of his kinsmen, yet they shall multiply across the desert.

[24] "And they shall raise their hand one against the other, against the Canaanites and the sons of Ishmael. Without mercy shall they slay them, invoking the name of a god to vindicate their madness. [25] Their enemies shall in like manner rise up against them, offering no quarter, for blood begets blood and fury begets fury. [26] An eye shall be given for an eye, and a tooth shall be demanded for a tooth. Such will be the way of things, since they have forsaken the way of wisdom. [27] Therefore shall wisdom forsake them in like manner, and the gods shall turn their backs on these people in disdain."

[28] At the appointed time, Abraham's son Isaac married his kinswoman Rebekah, the daughter of Bethuel. [29] And his elder son Ishmael took to himself two wives, casting aside the first because she failed to honor his father, but keeping the other close to him because she did what was right in the sight of Abraham.

[30] And in the course of time did Sarai breathe her last, whereupon Abraham drew Hagar back to himself. [31] It therefore came to pass that she bore him more sons, six in number, but each of them he sent away from him. For they chastened him, saying, "You do not honor the gods, and have turned your back on wisdom!" [32] But he stood against them, saying, "These gods of which you speak are only idols. Get behind me if you will not honor me!" And with this did he send them away into the east. [33] It is said that he built a city to contain them, with walls so high that the sun

could not be seen there.

³⁴ But the son of one of them, Epher, he appointed the general of his armies. ³⁵ Epher led these armies against the men of Libya and subdued them, and he spilled their blood without mercy and the blood of their children without quarter. ³⁶ Thus did it come to pass as the gods had reckoned, that blood would be shed by the kinsmen of Abraham. And this was but the beginning of their bloodletting.

³⁷ Abraham by no means saw the end of it, for in the course of days, he breathed his last.

7

¹ Never had there been a time like this in all of Egypt. The great empire that had built the pyramids lay subdued by an invader. ² The shepherd kings, they called them, for Abraham and his people had arrived as shepherds in the Nile Valley, cast aside the once-great pharaohs and made themselves lords of the delta. ³ The grandson of Abraham was Yacob-Har, which is "Jacob, the Horus." He reigned during his lifetime in the land of the pharaohs.

⁴ And in Babylon there rose up a king named Ammurapi, who served the sun god Shamash. From this god he claimed to have received the tablets of the law, by which he governed his empire.

⁵ And on an island in the Sea at the Center of the World, a king ascended the throne of Minos.

⁶ Seasons passed and the spokes of heaven's wheel

shifted in the sky. The stargazers marked the signs and wonders in the velvet skies overhead, and they took note of the changes in the seasons. [7] The Thebans from the highlands of Egypt, the ancient land of the pharaohs, chafed mightily beneath the Shemites from the north, for they were yet vassals to the sons of Abraham, who demanded of them taxes and tribute. [8] And the Shemites built for themselves a great capital in the lowlands, and they called its name Avaris.

[9] Now the greatest of these pharaohs was Apophis, who reigned forty years over the land and was among the last of Hyksos "the shepherd kings." [10] He was also called Auserre in the tongue of Egypt — that is, in his own tongue, Israel — for it is from him that the nation of Israel was born. [11] In his day, he amassed great wealth, trading with the kings of Minos to the north in the midst of the sea. [12] Such were his riches that the name of his capital was transferred to the tongue of the Romans, who called their word for greed "avarus." [13] And he worshipped only Seth, constructing a temple at Avaris that he consecrated in the great god's name. [14] Is it not written concerning him, "He chose for his patron the god called Seth. And he worshipped no other god in all the land, save for Seth alone"?

[15] And the Elohim in Canaan despaired at this, for Apophis worshipped not the god of their choosing. [16] Therefore did they say, "He has made himself our adversary!" [17] It is for this reason that the name Seth was perverted upon their lips to the name of Satan, which has that very meaning. And he was known also as the adversary

of the Horus kings in the south, which is to say the city of Thebes.

¹⁸ Indeed, the Elohim were not the only men who opposed Apophis. ¹⁹ The Thebans and their leader, Kamose by name, complained bitterly of the tribute paid to the shepherd king.

²⁰ "I should know how my strength is served, when one chieftain rules in Avaris and another in Ethiopia," he declared. ²¹ "Here I sit between an Asiatic and a Nubian, each in possession of a slice of Egypt! No man can find rest from the desolation that is wrought in the name of Seth."

²² His counselors, however, entreated him against any rash action, for they knew the strength of Apophis and the vengeance he would take upon them should they rise up to oppose Avaris.

²³ "Behold," they said, "all are loyal to the Asiatics as far south as Cusae. We are tranquil in our portion of Egypt. ²⁴ Elephantine is strong to the south, and the heart of the nation is with us north to Cusae. ²⁵ Men till for us the finest of their lands. Our cattle pasture in among the papyrus reeds. ²⁶ Corn is sent for our swine, and our cattle are not taken from us."

²⁷ But Kamose would not be swayed. In his anger did he raise an army to assail Apophis and his minions, saying, "No man can settle down when despoiled by the taxes of these men from Asia! ²⁸ Therefore shall I contend with him, that I may rip open his belly! May I deliver Egypt and smite the Asiatics!"

[29] Yet it was not to be. The armies of Kamose were driven back, and Avaris remained secure. Indeed, Kamose himself was slain.

[30] And the land did prosper. For seven years, the cattle of Egypt grew fat as they grazed in the fields of the delta. [31] Grain sprouted up, more plentiful than the rushes in the Sea of Reeds. The mighty Nile rushed forth each year at the inundation, overtopping its banks and blessing the soil with life abundant. [32] The sons of Egypt blessed Osiris for this bounty; and Apophis gave thanks to Seth, the keeper of storms, for visiting the earth with such abundance.

[33] It was at this time that Apophis appointed for himself a vizier, whom he placed over all the land. This one, like the pharaoh, was a Sethite from the seed of Abraham. [34] For he said to himself, "It is good that a kinsman should look after my abundance."

[35] This man's name was Yusuf, meaning "he that increases," and the scribes would call him Joseph.

[36] And this is how Yusuf came to be exalted in pharaoh's court.

[37] It came to pass that Apophis sought out Yusuf for his counsel, for he was known for his wisdom and discernment. Therefore did Auserre summon his kinsman to himself.

[38] And Yusuf came into the presence of Apophis, and he said to the king of Eygpt, "Behold, you have been granted many years of great prosperity. But times of bounty are ever followed by times of want. [39] Shall this time of plenty extend beyond the seventh year? If not, then what

shall become of you? ⁴⁰ Behold, seven years of abundance may give way to seven years of drought and famine. Then how shall you feed the people? ⁴¹ Therefore, let the pharaoh appoint a wise man to guard the land, and let him appoint also stewards of the grain in its abundance. ⁴² Charge these men to collect for the pharaoh one-fifth of all the harvest during these years of bounty, that this might be preserved for the lean years ahead. ⁴³ In this way the land shall not be laid waste by a famine, and the people of Egypt shall have plenty while others are in want."

⁴⁴ Apophis hearkened to Yusuf's counsel, and it was pleasing to his ears. ⁴⁵ Therefore did he appoint Yusuf to oversee the land of Egypt and its bounty. ⁴⁶ He placed a signet ring on his finger and arrayed him in fine garb, with a gold chain around his neck and a chariot driver at his command. ⁴⁷ And Apophis betrothed him to the daughter of Potiphera, a priest of On, which the Greeks call Heliopolis. (Now Potiphera means "dedicated to Ra," the sun god, and On was the city of the sun). ⁴⁸ It was then that Yusuf's name was called Osarseph, which means "he who magnifies Osiris."

⁴⁹ And Yusuf went out from the court of the pharaoh and into all the land of Egypt, collecting grain from the farmers and householders, and building great storehouses wherein it might be housed. ⁵⁰ The grain he gathered was like the sand of the sea; so plentiful was it that the record-keepers could not account for it all. ⁵¹ And in addition to this, he had his servants carve out a canal from the mighty Nile to the Fayyum Oasis to the west of it. There was water

captured, that it might provide a reserve when the rains were wanting.

⁵² And behold, in the course of seven years, it came to pass as Yusuf had predicted. ⁵³ The rains fell not in the highlands, and the waters of the Nile drew back. The inundation came not, and the land grew cracked and barren. ⁵⁴ Heads of grain fell from withered stalks, and the lifeless soil spurned them. ⁵⁵ Cattle grew lean, for there was nothing to graze on, and men grew restless, saying, "What shall become of us?"

⁵⁶ It was then that Yusuf opened the storehouses. It was then that he threw wide the doors to the granaries. And he said to the people, "Come forth! Partake! And enjoy the fruits of the bounty you once sacrificed!"

8

¹ In those days the famine was severe throughout the earth, even beyond the land of Egypt. And all the world came to the storehouses of Yusuf to buy grain. ² In this way was the house of the pharaoh enriched. And in this way was Yusuf's name magnified in all the earth. ³ And the people called him Zaphenath-Paneah, which means, "the one who nourishes the world with life."

⁴ But the pharaoh grew disconsolate, for he was ever aware that the Thebans sought his throne. ⁵ He therefore summoned to himself a seer, and he said to him, "You are able to see the gods, as though you yourself were one of them. ⁶ Am I not king of Egypt? Yet my visions are no

match for yours. ⁷ Teach me, therefore, how it is that you see so clearly the realms of heaven, that I may walk with the gods as you do." For he sought a sign from heaven, that he might guard himself against the Thebans.

⁸ The seer therefore said to him, "You must purify Avaris of the Thebans, for they are as lepers among us. If they conspire against you, and rise up from within, how shall you guard yourself against them? ⁹ Nay, let them be gone from this place and send them out into the quarries beyond the river. There they shall work to preserve your throne, and may not overthrow it. ¹⁰ In these quarries they can mine stones to build a wall around Avaris. Such a bulwark can guard against their brethren should they rise against you from the south."

¹¹ And the pharaoh hearkened to the seer's words. So he appointed Yusuf to the task of raising new walls around the city, should the king of the south rise up against him. ¹² For though Kamose, lord of Thebes, had fallen, a new king had risen to take his place. This was the brother of Kamose, whose name was Ahmose (but in the Greek tongue, Moses). ¹³ It he now set his mind to lead an army against Avaris and to drive out the Shemites from that place, for which reason he might be known as "the liberator" of his people.

¹⁴ When news of this reached Avaris, Yusuf hurried to complete the walls, redoubling the burden on the Thebans in the quarries. ¹⁵ And he sent word to the Elohim in Salem, saying, "Make haste to bring your armies hither, for our enemies the Thebans stand ready to assail us." ¹⁶ And

the Elohim heard him, and sent their emissaries to meet with him, for though they honored Yah, whom they called Yahweh, and the men of Avaris followed Seth, still they were of one blood. ¹⁷ The leaders of the Shemites from Canaan came down and appeared before Yusuf.

¹⁸ Now the famine was yet upon their land, and the shepherds from Canaan knew of the storehouses that Yusuf had built. ¹⁹ When, therefore, they appeared to him, they told him of their want, saying, "We have come down to you from Canaan to purchase food."

²⁰ But Yusuf accused them, saying, "You are spies! You have come down to see where our land is unprotected!"

²¹ He said this to test them, for he knew that Ahmose was eager to prevail against Avaris, and that he would certainly send spies before him.

²² And the shepherds answered and said to him, "We are brothers who lead the people of Canaan. Only one of our brethren has not joined with us, but remains in the land of our fathers."

²³ But Yusuf heeded this not, for he was wary. He therefore demanded that they should summon to him the one who had stayed behind, that Yusuf might know he was no Theban. ²⁴ And he said to them, "I judge that you are spies. Therefore shall you be tested in this manner. As the pharaoh lives, you shall not depart from this place until this 'brother' of yours comes forward. ²⁵ Send one of your number to retrieve him; if you do not, your words shall be revealed as falsehood."

²⁶ He then put them all in custody for three days. And

when these had passed, he gave them their freedom; only one was to remain as a guarantee that they should return to him with their countryman. ²⁷ It therefore came to pass that, in due course, they returned to him with their 'brother,' and Yusuf believed their words. ²⁸ Then did they pledge to him thousands of fighting men, that they might gain in exchange for this both provision and sanctuary within the land of Avaris.

To this they all agreed.

²⁹ In those days also, Apophis sought to fortify himself further against the Thebans by striking an alliance with Ethiopia to the south. By so doing, he reasoned, the Theban king would be caught in a vise between Apophis' forces to the north and the Ethiopians to the south.

³⁰ He therefore invited Queen Tany of Sheba, who ruled all Ethiopia and the south, to his palace in Avaris. This invitation she accepted, bringing with her gold and precious gemstones and spices from the land of Punt, which she bore with her in a great caravan up from the source of the Nile.

³¹ She brought with her also difficult questions, seeking to measure whether an alliance with Apophis was truly in her interest and that of her kingdom. For she reasoned that the Thebans stood directly across her northern border and might begin a campaign against her should she cast her lot with the northerners. ³² Would Apophis be able to protect her in such an instance? This question was in her mind, though not directly on her lips.

³³ In answer, Apophis showed her the great palace he

had built and the temple with its precincts and all the splendor of Avaris. [34] He made an offering for her in the temple he had built and set forth a great banquet in his honor, so that she saw no recourse but to form an alliance with him, saying, "I did not believed the words that were spoken of this place and its wonders until my own eyes beheld them. [35] Now it is plain that the half was not told to me, for your wisdom and prosperity exceeds all the praise that formerly reached my ears."

[36] Thereupon they made an agreement of alliance, and the queen returned to her own land.

[37] When Ahmose, however, heard of these things, and that the king of Avaris was mustering an army to defend against him, he went down to Ethiopia with his own men and gained an audience with the queen. [38] On his journey southward, there are those who say his forces were confronted by an army of serpents, and that he expelled these from the Ethiopian capital with the help of a great flock of ibises. [39] In truth, however, the serpents were soldiers in the service of Apophis (whose own name is also that of a great sky serpent), and they were defeated by men who fought under the sign of the ibis, which is sacred to the great god Thoth.

[40] This god was said to have created Amen, the mighty god to whom Ahmose had sworn allegiance and whose name was the last word on the lips of every prayer in Thebes. [41] In the names of these gods, Ahmose expelled the forces of Apophis and occupied the Ethiopian capital, which was Sheba. [42] In the wake of his victory, Ahmose

persuaded the men of that place to forswear the queen's pact with Avaris and renew their former alliance with Thebes. [43] This pact he sealed by marrying the queen herself.

[44] Then did he call upon them to offer them provision and to guard his borders as he marched against Avaris, to which they also consented.

[45] Once he had secured his southern border, Ahmose gathered his fighting men to him, many thousand in number. And they marched northward into the land of the pharaoh.

[46] From Thebes, they made their way down the Nile to Abydos, to Hermopolis and past the Fayyum to the sacred city of Heliopolis. Then they entered Heliopolis and laid hold of it, and brought it to heel. [47] Then did they advance upon the fortress of Sile and assail it with a single purpose. For this fortress guarded the border between Egypt and the land of Canaan. [48] By capturing it, he sought to cut off the Shemites of Avaris from their brethren to the north and east.

[49] In the course of time, the fortress fell. From that time forward, no more aid reached Yusuf from the shepherds of Canaan.

9

[1] Then did Ahmose send his emissary to the pharaoh there with this message: "Behold, you have held my people in your power for too long! [2] Release my countrymen from

the quarries beyond the river. Submit before the power of my armies. [3] Surrender, and I shall be lenient. But if you refuse, the Nile shall run red with blood. Therefore I demand this of you: Let my people go!"

[4] But the pharaoh's heart was hard against him, and he refused the demands of Ahmose.

[5] Instead did Apophis call forth to himself his son, Danaus, instructing him to assemble a fleet of great ships that they might fight the Thebans on the water. [6] For the king of Avaris had allied himself with the people of the Phoenix, in symbol of which the seafarers flew two banners: one of the eagle, or the phoenix, which was their own, and the other bearing the serpent of Apophis. [7] These seafarers had ports in Minos on the isle of Crete, whence they set sail around the central sea.

[8] Now Ahmose sent a second message to Apophis, proposing a treaty between them, and that his own son marry the daughter of Danaus. [9] But to this Apophis did not agree, for he knew that it was Ahmose's son who would be heir to the kingdom should he accept it.

[10] Therefore did Ahmose besiege Avaris, and he spilled the blood of its defenders into the river, as he had pledged. [11] His men slaughtered the livestock of the shepherds and left it as testament to their assault. [12] Yet still Avaris would not yield to the invaders. Still Ahmose could not capture it, so he withdrew.

[13] Then again did he send his emissary to the pharaoh, and again he demanded of him: "Let my people go!"

But again, the pharaoh refused him.

[14] It was then that the belly of the earth grew restless. In the north, in the nation of Minos, it rumbled from the depths of the underworld. [15] It churned in the forge of Hephaestus. And the Minoans trembled greatly at the sound of it, until it rose up out of its earthen vaults and broke forth on the surface of the land. [16] The mountain on the isle of Thera became as if alive, spewing smoke and breathing fire. [17] Appearing as a dragon bent on vengeance, its wrath overtook men in chariots as though standing still and crushed them like ants under bootheel.

[18] The skies drew dark and thick with smoke, and this smoke spread far and wide from Knossos, the capital of Minos, to Avaris and beyond to the ends of the earth. [19] The land of Egypt was plagued with infestations. [20] Frogs rose up and covered the land, but it would not bear them. [21] Gnats and flies were loosed upon the land, drawn by the carcasses of the Shemite herds and the bodies of the frogs that were now dying.

[22] Then the army of Thebans laid siege once again to proud Avaris, and a second time were the Thebans repulsed.

[23] Yet again did Ahmose demand of them, "Let my people go!"

And again did they refuse him.

[24] So Ahmose sent his men forward to slaughter what remained of the shepherds' livestock. Neither goat nor lamb nor calf was spared. [25] Smoke from the fiery mountain overtook the entire land, so that the people were afflicted by boils upon their skin. [26] Ash descended upon them like

hail from the sky, which was darkened as if a curtain had been drawn across the sun. [27] Locusts also rose up in mighty clouds as thick as a sandstorm from the red desert, so that no man could see his hand before him or the face of the man beside him.

[28] And the people of Avaris were sore afraid, for they thought themselves cursed of heaven. [29] Were these plagues not the work of the Egyptian sorcerers, who commanded serpents without being bitten and preserved the lives of the sleeping? [30] Could such men not have brought these plagues down upon the people?

[31] But the pharaoh would not yield to their fears, saying, "Behold, my heart is set against them. Have my people not resisted the Thebans in the past? Have they not repelled them? Shall it not be the same again?"

[32] It therefore came to pass that Ahmose attacked a third time, but a third time was he repulsed by proud Avaris.

[33] Then did he seek out a meeting with the pharaoh, that they might speak face to face without pretense. And the Shemite did accept this, for he thought that Ahomse intended to surrender. [34] But when the Theban arrived there, he bent not the knee before Avaris. [35] Nay, he dared look the pharaoh directly in his eye and said to him, "You have defied the will of Egypt and the gods in heaven for too long, false king. [36] Therefore, I say to you these last words: At midnight tonight, if you have not surrendered, I shall slay all your firstborn sons — from your own to the sons of your servants to the lambs and the calves that

remain in your fields. [37] This I swear in the name of the gods in heaven. Then and only then shall I depart this wretched place."

[38] At these words, the king was silent. He had repulsed this army of Thebans three times; now, he vowed, he would do so a fourth. [39] He therefore turned his back to Ahmose and departed, saying to his officers, "These men are fools, and stubborn. We shall teach them not to trifle with the sons of fortune!"

[40] That night did Ahmose send assassins into the streets of Avaris. In stealth did they pass through the city, messengers of death to the people who dwelt there. [41] The sons of Egyptians therein were spared, but the sons of the Shemites were slaughtered without mercy. [42] Yusuf was among the slain, and Ahmose did gather his bones as a testimony to the gods, and did carry them with him as he fought the enemy. [43] Amid the chaos did the Theban army move forward, butchering all those who stood in their way. [44] The defenders, stricken by grief as their sons lay fallen, stood helpless before the weapons of Ahmose, who stood at the head of his army crying, "Let my people go!"

[45] Then the pharaoh abandoned Avaris, and he fell back to Tanis with the remnants of his army. [46] Thence did they flee to the home of their kin, the land of Canaan, and many of the common people went with them, but they were pursued across the desert by the fury of Ahmose. [47] They passed through the Reed Sea to escape him and sought refuge in the desert places of Sinai. [48] And it is said that the storms of Seth watched over them, passing before them in

a pillar of cloud by day and a pillar of light blazing down from the heavens in the night.

⁴⁹ But the ships of the Phoenix could not follow them there in the marshes, and could offer no support for the fleeing armies. Therefore they sailed forth to find refuge, both from the Theban pharaoh and from the wrath spewed forth by the dragon beneath the mountain Thera.

⁵⁰ Danaus himself, however, fled north to the city of Argos, which likewise became known for its ships, while others still rode the winds westward, founding new colonies along the sea's south coast. ⁵¹ These were the cities of Utica and Tangier, of Sabratha and Tipaza, and many others.

⁵² Others in the fleet of the Phoenix sailed to the eastward shores of the central sea, where they founded the kingdom of Dan. But they did remain in their ships, as it is written in the book called Judges.

⁵³ The name Dan in a certain tongue means "judge," and Canaan, the name of the land where they settled, means "merchant" — for they were sea merchants. ⁵⁴ Their cities there were and Tripoli and Baaelbek, Beru and Arqa and Ashkelon, Acre and Sidon and nearby Dan Jaan. The last of these means "Dan of the Woodlands."

⁵⁴ Some say it was thence that an expedition set forth westward, passing over the central sea to its farthest reaches and beyond before coming ashore at last on an island greener still than their homeland. ⁵⁵ And this, some say, is why they were called the Whelps of the Wood that Does Not Whither, as it is written also, "Dan is a lion's

whelp."

⁵⁶ They called themselves the Danites or the Danaan, and the goddess Dana was their mother.

10

¹ Some of the Shemites who fled by land surrendered to Ahmose, while others continued onward toward the land of Canaan.

² To those who joined with Ahmose he gave new laws — the laws of the Thebans — but he gave them no provision as they passed through the desert, as he sought to test their will. ³ They therefore grumbled against him, saying to themselves, "It would have been better had we died in Egypt. In that place, we had all the food we wanted. ⁴ We had pots of meat that nourished us as we sat around about them. But see? Our new master has brought us into this desert that we might starve to death!"

⁵ So Ahmose gave them bread to eat in the mornings, and told them in the evenings, "You may hunt for your own food!" ⁶ There was quail in that place, so they brought it back to themselves for sustenance. ⁷ He told them not to store up the bread among them, but some of them paid no heed to him. For had not Yusuf taught them well to preserve their grain in the storehouse? ⁸ Yet they had no proper place to preserve it, and it became putrid and infested with maggots, so they could not eat it. ⁹ And Ahmose was wroth with them for wasting their provision.

[10] But the people grew restless and thought to themselves, "We are now far from Egypt. Come, therefore, let us choose leaders from among us to challenge this false pharaoh, that we might prevail against him and return again to Avaris!" [11] To lead them they chose a certain Korah, son of Kohath, and at his side were two others name Abiram and Dathan. [12] These took counsel together, preparing to rise up against Ahmose, but he became aware of it and called Dathan and Abiram to him to give account.

[13] Yet they answered and said to him, "We shall heed not your summons. You have brought us here from a land flowing in milk and honey, and now you seek to kill us in the wilderness! [14] Would you treat us as slaves? Nay, we shall not come!"

[15] Then Korah gathered his followers to him that they might rise up against Ahmose. [16] They were two hundred and fifty in number. Yet were they no match for the army of Ahmose, which set upon them with such fury that it seemed the very earth had opened up to consume them. [17] After this did Ahmose root out every rebel, and those he knew had grumbled against them. [18] He slaughtered them without mercy, as a plague sweeps down to slay man, woman and child. Fourteen thousand of them fell in the wake of the rebellion, before Ahmose was content.

11

[1] In those days did Ahmose pursue the Shemites as far as the banks of a certain river. [2] Next to the Nile, it was but

a stream. Beside the mighty Euphrates, it was only a trickle. But Ahmose did not cross it in pursuit of those who had fled him. ³ These, the Shemites, found succor with the Elohim in the city of Salem, which is also called Jerusalem. ⁴ But Ahmose and his forces continued northward, where he subdued the armies of the Syrians as far as Byblos.

⁵ Over the land of Canaan he appointed one of his own generals, Hoshea, whom the scribes have named as Joshua and whom the Greeks know as Jesus. ⁶ He was called the son of Nun, the Egyptian god of the ancient waters from which all things sprang forth. This is because he hailed from Hermopolis in Egypt, the sacred city of this god.

⁷ The men made a pledge to Ahmose that they would follow Hoshea as they had followed their pharaoh. And they said to Hoshea, "Whoever rebels against your word and heeds it not, howsoever you may command them, shall be put to death!" ⁸ So they invaded the land and laid waste many cities. For Hoshea had given them this charge: "When you come upon a city of Canaan, lay siege to it and show no mercy. ⁹ Slaughter every living thing therein, the fighting men, their women and their children. Spare not their herds and flocks, but take only the gold and silver, that in so doing we might enrich the king's treasury."

¹⁰ He gave this order because he had seen the rebellion of Korah, and he wished to have no part of the Shemites' rebellions. ¹¹ And the men of Thebes did as they were bidden. They slaughtered every fighting man, their women and their children. They spared not the flocks of the Shemites, nor their herds. But they took only the gold and

silver, and thus did they enrich the pharaoh's treasury. [12] In this manner was Canaan laid to waste, and so were the Shemites were utterly crushed.

[13] But Salem withstood Hoshea's armed men, and did not yield before them.

[14] It was there, in Salem, that many of those from Avaris had sought refuge. And the Elohim who were on the council there received them. [15] The city itself belonged to the Jebusites, a tribe of Shemites who had built a mountain fortress which they called Zion. [16] These people were known as "the threshers." Some say this was because they harvested grain from the fields, after the manner of Cain; they would crush and winnow it on the threshing floor. [17] Others say it is because they were fierce warriors who were able to beat down their enemies after the manner of threshers.

[18] And the refugees came before the Elohim and said to them, "How shall we stand against the Egyptians? They have driven us from our homes, killed our firstborn sons and butchered all who stood against them."

[19] And the Elohim said to them, "Which gods do you serve?"

[20] They said, "We honor Seth, the god of our king and our city."

[21] Now the Elohim remembered their fathers in Eden, and the recalled how Seth had opposed them in Aratta. [22] These who stood before now them were kinsmen. Yet the men from Avaris had been deceived, or so did the Elohim reason. [23] For was not Seth as crafty as a serpent?

Had he not deceived them from the beginning?

²⁴ Therefore did the Elohim say to them, "Where is your king? And what has become of your city."

²⁵ And they answered, saying, "Our king is departed from us, we know not whence, and our city is in ruins."

²⁶ Then the Elohim said, "Behold, has not your god abandoned you?"

²⁷ But they said, "Truly, he did go before us in the desert, riding the clouds by day and casting down fire in a pillar by night."

²⁸ "Nay," said the councilors. "This was not Seth, but the god Yahweh, whom we worship. He is lord of the storms and the highest heights. He has sanctified this mountain where you stand, for which reason you are safe here."

²⁹ And they knew not what to say to this.

³⁰ "Behold, he has brought you out of Egypt that you might join with us, your kinsmen. And this shall be your homeland, a land of milk and honey. ³¹ Curse not the name of Ahmose, for it was by Yahweh's hand that he delivered you from the evil one — from your false god Seth, who forsook you, as ever he is wont to do. ³² This Seth is but a trickster, and has been so since the beginning. He tempted your fathers in the garden and caused them to rise up against Yahweh. ³³ A curse is upon him and all who hail him. From this curse has Ahmose liberated you, for which reason he is your savior as well."

³⁴ The men from Avaris looked hard at one another. "Then are you his servants as well?"

[35] But the Elohim answered, "We serve only Yahweh. His hand moves in ways that surpass reckoning. We honor his ways, which are beyond our understanding. Be thankful, therefore, that Ahmose has delivered you."

12

[1] Then did the scribes of the Elohim, in the years ahead, set forth a new history of the fight out of Egypt. Therein was Ahmose transformed from invader to deliverer. [2] His name they gave as Moshe, which the Greeks render as Moses. And his Theban heritage was stricken from memory, that he might become a Hebrew in the minds of the people.

[3] To accomplish their purpose, they drew upon the tale of Sargon, wherein his mother bore him in secret and cast him as an infant into a river, secure in an ark of rushes and bitumen. [4] So it was now, too, with Moses. The scribes of the Elohim set forth a tale wherein he was born in secret by a Hebrew woman. [5] And just as the mother of Sargon had done to him, the mother of Moses did to her infant in like manner. She placed him in a basket sealed with pitch and set him adrift upon the river.

[6] And behold, it came to pass that he was drawn out of the waters by the daughter of the pharaoh. [7] Just as Sargon had been raised by a man called Akki the Water Drawer, so Moses in the same way was drawn out of the water. [8] And some say it was for this reason that the Elohim called him

"Moses," for they recalled that it was similar to the Hebrew word for "drawing out." [9] In this manner did they complete their deception. [10] In their tale was Ahmose made a Hebrew, having been transformed through the tale of Sargon into an adopted son of the Theban pharaoh.

[11] Then did the Elohim make laws for themselves and place them upon his lips. [12] They remembered the manner in which Hammurabi, the king of Babylon, ascended a great mountain to receive the words of the law from the great god Shamash. [13] They recalled that this law had been inscribed upon a tablet of stone and displayed for all to see, and they wove a tale in the likeness of this history to fit their story of Moses. [14] In it did he ascend the mountains of Sinai and receive the code from Yahweh. In it did he deliver it to the people, saying, "All that Yahweh has commanded, these things shall we do."

[15] In this way did the Elohim place the words of their law into the mouth of their god, and of Moses, that they might themselves hold sway over the people. [16] They demanded that the people should worship no other god save Yahweh, and that they should make no graven image for themselves, lest Yahweh's wrath be kindled against them.

[17] "For behold," they warned the people, "Yahweh your god is a jealous god, and his wrath is a consuming fire. [18] Hearken therefore to the warning he utters: Each man who defies him shall receive recompense for his folly; and not the man alone, but his children and his children's children. [19] So shall they be cursed, even to the third and

fourth generation because they have defied the will of Yahweh."

[20] These were the decrees of the Elohim: That every man among the people should relinquish the firstborn of their flocks and their household to Yahweh's service; that they should never appear in his presence empty-handed; and that they must dedicate the first fruits of their soil to his storehouse. [21] That the man who defies his parents, be they just or unjust, should be stoned. That a virgin not pledged to another must marry the man who takes her by force. [22] That a woman who defends her husband by striking his rival's loins should have her hand cut off, and that she be shown no pity.

[23] These laws did they craft to their own ends, that the ancient ways of Osiris might be lost. That the true laws might be obscured. [24] These were the laws of Enoch, which had been hidden from the eyes of men by the Elohim; which had been stored within an ark from days of old. [25] There were those who remembered these things and said, "What has been done with the ark of our covenant? Where have the writings of the ancients been hidden?"

[26] So the Elohim crafted for themselves a new ark, which they adorned with gold. And the ark they built was fashioned after the manner of the ark in which they had slain Osiris.

[27] Thus did they command their workmen: "Build for us therefore an ark of acacia wood, and let these be its dimensions: It is to be in length two cubits, and in breadth one cubit and one-half, which shall also be its height.

[28] Adorn it and line it in the purest gold, and fashion gold molding around about it.

[29] "Cast four rings of gold, one for each of the ark's four feet. Fashion also poles of acacia wood, and cover them likewise in gold. [30] These shall be inserted into the four rings, that you may bear the ark from place to place. And they are not to be removed. They shall, henceforth, remain within the golden rings. [31] Now fashion also for the ark a seat of atonement to be placed atop it, and create from gold the image of two figures, placing the first at one end of the ark and the second at its opposite side. Their wings shall extend toward the heavens, that they might overshadow the ark's covering."

[32] And the two winged figures were fashioned in likeness of the twin goddesses, Isis and Nephthys. For they reasoned, "Behold, this shall be a sign to all our enemies. When we march out against them, the ark shall go before us. [33] They shall witness the power of the pharaohs in its craftsmanship. And they shall cower and run in fear from us, thinking the armies of Egypt are upon them."

[34] In this way did they violate their own law against graven images. Yet they cared not.

[35] And when the people asked them yet again, "What has been done with the ark of our covenant?" the Most High of the Elohim said, "Behold! It is here before you. [36] And within it lies the ark of Yahweh's covenant with his people, which he entrusted to Moses: the same covenant that was handed down in Eden and lost by the folly of Seth and his minions. [37] Now it has been found and restored to

us, that we might know and dwell in the presence of the one true god."

38 And the people looked, and marveled.

39 But one among them stepped forward and said to the Most High, "We would see the tablets with our own eyes, that we may know they are secure."

40 And the Most High answered and said to him, "Do you dare challenge Yahweh your god? Know you not that the ark is his very throne? Would you therefore command him to step down that you might test him? 41 No! For you are but mortal flesh, unfit to bind the straps of his sandals! Never shall you gaze upon the sacred stones of Moses. 42 If you so much as stretch out your hand to steady the ark when the oxen stumble, you shall perish on the spot. 43 Woe to you, unworthy wretch! These tablets were forged by the finger of Yahweh, whose face no man may gaze upon and whose mind no man may know."

44 The one who had stepped forward was silent. And the ones who had unspoken doubts stepped backward. 45 No more did they dare to challenge the Most High, and the ark remained sealed before them.

45 What lay within, no man knew. And when it came about one day that the ark was lost to them, no man fathomed what had become of it. 46 Such is the way of deception. It survives only so long as a deceiver preserves it, until it vanishes from the sight of men like a wisp of smoke in the mists of morning.

13

¹ The Elohim laid their yoke upon the people and did warn them. Words of fury they spoke to them, words of terror and foreboding.

² Through their laws did the Elohim amass great power, drawing into their treasuries vast wealth by the word of their decree. ³ The people chafed beneath their edicts, but dared not challenge them, for these laws were the words of their god, and those who dared question them would remain not long among the living.

⁴ For the Elohim spoke thus to the Shemites of Canaan: "The prophet or dreamer who speaks against Yahweh shall be slain. You must purge the evil from among you."

⁵ And again: "The one who displays contempt for a priest or judge who is the minister of Yahweh shall be slain. You must purge the evil from among you."

⁶ These were the wages of their iniquity. These would be the penalties for rebellion. ⁷ The Elohim heaped threat upon threat, and indignity upon indignity, as they brought oppression to the people. ⁸ No freedom would they grant the men in thrall to them. No quarter did they give those who defied them.

⁹ "If any man should defy the word of Yahweh, he shall be cursed among all men. He shall be cursed in the city and cursed, likewise, in the country. His basket shall be cursed, and his kneading trough shall be cursed. ¹⁰ Hear this now, you women! The fruit of your womb shall be cursed. ¹¹ And

hear this now, you men! The crops of the field, and the calves of your herds and the lambs of your flocks shall bear the curse of Yahweh. [12] When you enter in shall you be cursed, and when you go out shall you be cursed.

[13] "Confusion shall assail you from every side, that all you attempt shall end in ruin. [14] Disease shall come upon you, and pestilence, until you are wiped from the face of the land you seek to possess. [15] There shall come upon you plague and fever, scorching heat and withering drought. [16] Blight shall overtake you and mold shall be found within your storehouse. [17] The sky shall be as bronze, and the earth shall be as iron. Rain will be turned to dust and powder, which shall fall from the skies until you are no more.

[18] "Your enemies shall rout you. You shall attack from one direction and flee from seven. [19] The carrion birds shall pick at your carcasses, and no one shall disperse them. [20] Your skin shall be covered in boils and sores, and your body filled with tumors; no relief shall you obtain from them. [21] And madness shall come upon you, blindness of the mind and of the eye, so that you grope in vain through the darkness. Yet the path shall elude you. [22] Robbers shall take what is yours, and no one shall deliver you.

[23] "Your wives shall be raped. Your homes shall stand empty. Your vineyards shall wither and be given to over to worms, and your oxen shall be slaughtered before your eyes. [24] Your ass, your sheep and even your children shall be taken from you. Locusts shall afflict you, and the foreigner shall rule over you, that you may be a cause for

ridicule among the nations. [25] These things shall surely come upon you, lest you obey the commands of your god, Yahweh."

[26] When the people heard these things, they were deeply afraid. And they dared not question. They dared not disobey. [27] It came to pass, therefore, that the Elohim gathered to themselves such power that they grew haughty, even beyond what they had been before. [28] And they said to themselves, "Come, let us impose our will upon all the land." And they sent the spies out into the land around about Salem that they might subdue it, and these brought back with them a favorable report.

[29] Therefore did they assemble an army, saying, "When you march out against a city to assail it, offer them peace if they submit to you. [30] Then shall they be as slaves to you. The work of their hands shall be done in your service, at your bidding, without complaint. [31] Yet if they will not be your slaves, but engage you in battle, lay siege then to that place. And when it is delivered into your hand, put every man therein to the sword. [32] Then take the women, the children and the livestock as plunder for yourselves.

[33] "Yet in the cities of the nations that Yahweh shall give to you, leave nothing alive there. [34] Spare them not a single breath, but annihilate the cities of the Hitties, the Amorites, the Canaanites, the Perizzites, the Hivites and the Jebusites. Utterly destroy them, lest they spread the filth of their gods and entice you to break the commandments of Yahweh."

[35] The point of the sword went forth before them, and bloodshed followed in their wake.

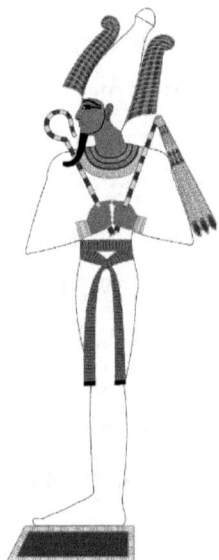

The Book of

Journeys

1

¹ The Pharaoh Ahmose was fruitful and prosperous, becoming the father of many children, and inaugurating a new and golden age in the land of Egypt. ² Ahmose reigned for ten and ten and five years again. He it was who outlawed the ritual of sacrifice to the gods, which the shepherd king Abram had sought to perform amid his fever and which other nations also undertook to practice in their madness.

² The line of Ahmose abode on the throne of Egypt for ten generations and beyond, honoring the gods Amen and Thoth with their regnal names. ³ From the seed of Ahmose sprang the first woman to sit upon the throne of the Two Lands, and Thutmose, the third of his name, who ruled more than two score and a dozen years. ⁴ As Ahmose had been "The Liberator," this Thutmose became known to his people as "The Warrior," leading the armies of Egypt into Canaan and Syria, across the Euphrates and south into Nubia.

⁵ His greatest victory was at Megiddo, in the famed battle of Armageddon. It was here that he defeated an army of Canaanites and Syrians led by the king of Kadesh and supported by the Mittani. ⁶ It was here that archers first drew bows of sinew, wood and horn crafted together.

⁷ When the armies of the pharaoh came upon them, the fighting men of Canaan took counsel and became convinced that Thutmose would lead his men along the roads on either side of the mountains of Megiddo. This was a longer route, but more certain. ⁹ The third way was directly through the mountains, by way of a narrow pass called Aruna where an army would be hemmed in on either side and forced to move ahead single-file.

¹⁰ Yet this was the way that Thutmose decided upon. Though his counselors sought to sway him, he was determined to take the most treacherous path. ¹¹ "I swear by the love Ra has shown me and by the favor that Amen has shown me that I shall proceed upon this road of Aruna. ¹² Shall my enemies, whom Ra detests, think of me,

'Behold, he has begun to fear us, for he takes another path'? For this will they surely think."

¹³ The Canaanites indeed believed that he would take the easier course and, in preparation, had stationed their armies on either side of the mountains. ¹⁴ But in the end, they were undone. The Egyptians burst forth upon them at the plain of Megiddo like water gushing from a narrow channel, forcing them to take refuge in the city and laying siege to it until the men inside gave themselves over to Thutmose.

¹⁵ As it is written, Thutmose "prevailed over them at the head of his army. At the sight of him coming forth, they fled in fear, rushing headlong toward Megiddo. ¹⁶ They left their horses and chariots of silver and gold, that they might be lifted up over the walls of the town by their garments. ¹⁷ Then were their chariots captured with great ease, as their ranks lay stretched out on their backs on the field of battle, as fish lie in the cords of a fisherman's net."

¹⁸ Thutmose captured not only Megiddo, but the lands around about it as well. The city of Kadesh fell to him, and the Mittani fled before him. Even the Elohim at Salem could not resist him. ¹⁹ So complete was his victory that it was, from that day forward, spoken of in whispers of dismay and vexation by the Elohim and those who served them. ²⁰ In the time that followed, Thutmose stretched forth his hand to subdue all of Canaan and Syria, eastward to the great Euphrates and beyond. ²¹ Those taken at the point of the sword or bound to subjugation remembered this battle as the end of a great era. ²² Their stories were

passed along for generations uncounted, until Megiddo came to be spoken as the name of an age's end.

²³ For the line of Ahmose, it marked not an end but a point of turning. From that time forward, no pharaoh of Egypt would rule as great an expanse as the empire Tuthmose surveyed. ²⁴ As is the way of things, kings go forth to conquer and return to ruin. The Two Lands prospered for a time yet, but there came a day that their splendor was not what it had been, and a new pharaoh came to the throne who was intent upon restoring it.

²⁵ This one, like his father and two others before him, was named Amenhotep, which translated means "Amen is content." ²⁶ But the pharaoh was not content, for he looked to the sky and beheld there a single god, not the many gods and goddesses of his fathers. ²⁷ This god shone down upon him, its radiance reflected in his own, and as he basked in the glory of this light, he became resolved within his heart to swear fealty to the one god who was its source.

²⁸ The young pharaoh dispatched the high priest of Amen to serve as overseer on a quarrying expedition, whereupon he himself seized control of the temples in the capital. ²⁹ It was not long before he had proscribed any worship of Amen. Even the very names of Amen and his consort Mut were removed from the temple precincts, which were both defaced and defiled. ³⁰ No festival was to be held in honor of any other god save the one god of radiance, called the Aten, and no images of theses gods were to be displayed.

³¹ Then, in a moment of inspiration and conceit, the

pharaoh discarded the name of his birth and took to himself a new title to honor the name of the Aten. [32] Henceforth would he be called Akhenaten, the living spirit of the Aten, manifested on the earth as light incarnate and the founder of a great new capital called the Aten's Horizon.

[33] He chose for the site of this new city a desert place. In this place there had been neither temple nor marketplace nor simple abode. [34] "Behold," said Akhenaten, "it is I, the pharaoh, who has found it, when it belonged to neither god nor goddess; when it was ruled by neither king nor queen; when it belonged not to any people. [35] My father, Hor-Aten, declared in my hearing, 'It is to be my own abode, the Horizon of the Aten eternally.'"

[35] On the banks of the Nile toward the sunrise it rose up from the desert, with a palace for the pharaoh in the north, temples to the Aten at its heart and estates for the great families at its southern edge.

[36] But the pharaoh placed upon the backs of his people a burden too great for them to bear. [37] They cowered in fear lest they be discovered honoring any other god save the Aten, and they hid the images of their own gods, careful that they should not be seen.

[38] Such is the way of things when one god rules by force of arms. It is the way of veiled truth and hidden honor; the way of fearful smiles, of two faces and two tongues. [39] When a general, priest or king places his own god on a stone pedestal, it is the people who become as stones, afraid to speak apart from what is accepted or act beyond

the measure of their masters.

2

[1] As Akhenaten turned his eyes inward to his new capital, he neglected the outward. A great plague swept down across the nation, so that thousands perished, and the power of his sun god could do nothing in the face of it. [2] The people cried out, yet their cries were not answered. They suffered, yet their suffering was not assuaged.

[3] Neither did the pharaoh answer the cries of his people from out of Canaan, the land which his fathers had subdued and made to serve them. [4] As the Hittite king grew in strength and boldness, he sought out an alliance with the Mittani, whose realm encompassed the headwaters of the great Tigris and Euphrates, sending to their king a statue of gold. [5] Yet this gold was but a gloss that covered a figure carved from wood.

[6] At this the Mittani king was offended, and the alliance with Egypt was strained. [7] In due course, the growing might of the Hittites was brought to bear against the Mittani, who could not stand alone against them. [8] Abandoned by Egypt, they were overrun, and the Hittite armies swept southward toward Canaan along the shore of the Sea at the Center of the World.

[9] Syria fell to the them, yet Akhenaten (whom the Greeks call Achencres) lifted not a hand to stay them. [10] The Hittites urged the men of Canaan to rise up against

the pharaoh whose fathers had subdued them, so that the men Akhenaten had favored with high office in that land cried out to him for succor. [11] The servant of Egypt who ruled in Jerusalem wrote in desperation to the capital, seeking help against the Hebrews who had risen against him. [12] These men, at the bidding of the Elohim, sought to throw of the yoke of the pharaoh and renew their own sovereignty in Canaan.

[13] Yet amidst the pleas of his own chosen governors, the pharaoh stood by, sending no help.

[14] Abdi-Heba, who had sworn allegiance to the pharaoh, was disconsolate. [15] "Why do you favor the Hebrews and oppose the rulers?" he asked. "We are bereft of troops in our garrison. [16] Oh, that the pharaoh should guard his lands! All the pharaoh's lands have entered into rebellion. [17] If only I might enter the presence of my king and look at him squarely with both eyes, yet alas, the enmity against me is strong and I am prevented. [18] May the pharaoh send troops for his garrison, that I may enter into his presence and fix my gaze upon him. [19] Then, as my lord lives, I would say to him, "Lost are the lands of the pharaoh. Do you not hear me? All your rulers are lost; the pharaoh, my lord, has not a single ruler left.

[20] "May the pharaoh set his gaze upon his archers, and may he send troops of bowmen, for the Hebrews sack the pharaoh's lands. [21] If archers are sent, his lands may be preserved, but if they do not come, all these lands shall be forfeit."

[22] Yet the pharaoh heeded him not, and did not reply.

Neither did he send archers, and so it was that the lands of Canaan and Syria were wrested from him.

[23] The Hittites, in their coming, took many men of Egypt who were in Canaan as their prisoners. [24] Yet their victory became a curse at the moment they grasped it, for the Egyptians were infected by the plague that had come upon them, and this they carried northward into the land of Hatti. [25] There it felled a great many, even Suppiluliuma, their monarch, as well as his heir.

[26] Nor was the pharaoh himself safe in his new capital. The golden rays of the Aten could not shield his family from the ravages of this vile affliction, nor could the remoteness of his new capital. [27] In the course of but a short time, his mother, three of his daughters and one of his wives were taken from him.

[28] In those days, it happened that the sea winds bore a prince across the seas to the land of Egypt. Some say he came from Greece and others from the high steppes beyond the inland sea. [29] And betaking himself to the capital, he was brought before the pharaoh himself.

[30] Now, it is said that this young man had fled his home country because his father, who was king of that land, had given him no title. [31] Therefore provoked to anger, he rose up and undertook a rebellion with the help of many cohorts. [32] Yet his uprising was not successful, and his father Nenius expelled him from the land owing to his acts of treason.

[33] When, therefore, he sought refuge in Egypt, there were those who eyed him warily, thinking he had come as a

pirate to raid that nation's treasures. ³⁴ For in those days were more and more men taking to the seas, plying the green waters of the central sea as if they were a font of ill-gotten wealth. ³⁵ Therefore did the Greek prince come to be called Gaythelos, or in the western tongue, Goídel Glas, which means "green raider."

³⁶ But when he was brought before the pharaoh, the daughter of the pharaoh was also there at court. ³⁷ This was the custom of Akhenaten, to rule with his family by his side, and his daughter was all the more precious to him now that her sisters had departed this life. ³⁸ The plague that had stricken them had not yet taken her, and the pharaoh had begun to despair of finding a way to shield her from its grip.

³⁹ When, therefore, his daughter and the Greek prince expressed a fondness for each other, it presented not a threat but an opportunity. ⁴⁰ Many were the whispers and suspicions in the capital concerning this newcomer: that he sought to plunder this rich new city or even that he sought the hand of the pharaoh's daughter as a means of supplanting Akhenaten. ⁴¹ It was unthinkable that such a one should be allowed to marry into the royal line and remain in Egypt, where he might plot to overthrow the pharaoh as he had schemed against his own father.

⁴² Yet, if he should one day return home to his own country and claim its throne, such an alliance would prove valuable. ⁴³ More than this, if he were to take the princess away from the wretched plague that was all about them, she would be preserved, along with the pharaoh's lineage.

[44] Akhenaten therefore agreed that they should wed, on the condition that Gaythelos should leave the country straightaway with his new bride and take her away to a safe distance, beyond the reach of the plague.

[45] To this did he consent, and shortly after they were wed did they make their departure, along with a retinue of ships well stocked with supplies and wares to trade as they ventured forth to their new home, wherever the waves might take them.

[46] But their departure did not safeguard the kingdom of Akhenaten, which was soon to be no more. [47] In the passing of a few years, the pharaoh himself was dead, and the generations that followed made certain that his great god suffered the same fate. [48] In a few short years, all record of Akhenaten and his ways were removed from the walls of the temples. [49] The priesthood of Amen was restored to its former glory, and the images of the Aten were removed. [50] His glorious capital sank back into the dusts of the desert, abandoned, and its pillars removed to build more temples to the glory of Amen and the old gods. [51] Akhenaten himself was all but forgotten, his name no longer uttered on the lips of the people and his countenance removed from the works of chiseled stone.

3

[1] In those days, the Elohim once again grew strong in Salem. Egypt had drawn back from out of Canaan, and the

Hittites were distant masters, having turned their eyes westward toward Anatolia and Greece.

² In place of the great empires there arose a wealth of city-states, tribes and petty kingdoms, and these were scattered across the land between the coastal plane and the river Jordan. ³ There were the Moabites and the Edomites in the south and east; the Philistines of Ashdod, Askelon and Gaza along the southern coast; and the Amalekites to the south of them.

⁴ Others among these principalities traced their lineage to the great shepherd pharaohs Maibre, called Abraham, and Yacob-har, named among them as Jacob. ⁵ Among these were the tribes of Judah and Benjamin, of Reuben, Gad, Asher, Naphtali, Simeon, Issachar and Zebulun.

⁶ One tribe boasted that it was descended from Yusuf, the great vizier of Apophis. But these did not follow Seth as their fathers had, for fear of the Elohim, and in strife was their tribe divided between two factions, called Ephraim and Mannasseh. ⁷ There was also a tribe of itinerant priests called Levi, who aligned themselves closely with the Elohim.

⁸ But the greatest among the tribes was Dan. The men of this tribe hearkened not to the priesthood in Jerusalem, which sought to yoke them, demanding, "Why does Dan linger by his ships?"

⁹ The people of Dan did not bend the knee to Jerusalam, nor did they crawl on their bellies before those who would ensnare them. ¹⁰ Their numbers were great in the land of Canaan, surpassed only by the sons of

Jerusalem and its territories. And their enmity was long set one against the other. [11] The men of Jerusalem assailed them on their southern coast, so that some among them moved northward and settled in the land called Laish, near the ports of Tyre and Sidon where their kinsmen dwelt.

[12] Tyre was found within the regions of Asher, the land of the goddess Asherah, she who treads upon the sea. [13] In Jerusalem were her sacred pillars torn down by the priests of the Elohim, but in the north were her shrines and altars guarded. [14] Some say that their name is the name of old for Osiris, that is Asar, and that the pillars they erected were an homage to his ways.

[15] During their migrations did the nobles of their race take this title for themselves, calling themselves Aesir, which means "lords."

[16] But because of the contempt that was borne them by the servants of Yawheh, they called the scion of Asher the son of a servant whore, and in so doing reviled the god who had turned from their wickedness. In like manner did they slander the Danites.

[17] The Elohim and their prophets would rail against them, saying, "I am against you, O Tyre, and I will cause many nations to come against you, as the sea sends forth its waves. [18] They shall lay to waste the walls of Tyre and cast her towers down, then shall I scrape away her rubble and leave only a bare rock. [19] To the sea shall she be consigned, and there shall she spread her fishnets, but on the shores shall her cities fall to the sword."

[20] And again: "Shall not the coastline tremble at the

sound of your downfall, at the groaning of the wounded and the slaughter that comes upon you? [21] I will make you a place of desolation, like a city where no one dwells. Then shall I call up depths of the ocean to wash over you and its unbounded waters to cover you. [22] Then shall I cause you to dwell in the nether regions of the earth, as in the ancient ruins, with the ones cast into the pit. Neither shall you return to reclaim your place of glory. [23] But I will make your end a horror and you will be no more. You shall be sought, but never again found."

[24] Nevertheless did the Danites thrive and prosper, setting forth on expeditions over land and sea. The former joined with some among the Asherites in embarking on a journey northward. [25] They passed by the land of Eden in Aratta, nearby Lake Van. Those who dwelt there were an ancient race, the Vanir, in a place they would remember as Vanaheimr, which means "the home of the Vanir."

[26] Moving on from that place, they traveled north at a further distance to the steppes beyond Axsaina, the Dark Sea, which is known to the Greeks as Pontus. [27] In this place they were called the Scythians, known as great riders of the horse who spread their herds far and wide across the plains.

[28] Thence did some travel northward and west along the river called Danube, to which they gave their name. [29] They did likewise navigate the waters of the Don and the Donets, the Dnieper and the Dniester, leaving their mark upon those places as well. [30] It was beyond the Don, to the east in Asia, that they built their great capital of Asgard,

that is "enclosure of the Aesir."

[31] To secure themselves, they charged their smiths with creating three great treasures. (They called their ironworkers dwarves because they were always stooped over as their hammers rang against the hot iron.) [32] The first of these treasures was a great boar with golden bristles, to symbolize courage and ferocity in battle. [33] The second was a golden armband, and the third was a hammer they named Mjolnir, which means "crusher." [34] This last, it is said, always returned to the one who wielded it, for that one was the mightiest in battle.

[35] Then, to defend their city, they pressed into service a certain man of great skill and stature, whose companion in the task was a great stallion. [36] As a reward for his work, he was promised the hand of a true goddess as a sign that he should be one of them if he were to complete the task by springtime. [37] The workhorse and its kind helped the craftsman and his servants move all the stones into their proper places, and it appeared that he would indeed achieve his goal. [38] But the Aesir were loath to welcome him into their company, so they set loose a mare before the craftsman's stallion, which then chased its quarry far into the fields. [39] Thus delayed, the man could not finish his task in the appointed number of days, and the Aesir slew him in recompense for his failure.

[40] Forgiveness was not the way of the Aesir, nor was mercy in their aspect. [41] Though their own name meant "lords" or "high ones" and was close akin to the name Asar — that is, Osiris — they had abandoned his ways and

made war on one another, as had the Elohim and their followers. [42] Their way was to sacrifice the lives of men to their gods, hanging them from a tree and piercing them through with their spears.

[43] Their master was named Odin, who had come from the city of Troy when it fell, and his armies made war upon the Vanir, whose own forces came northward and laid siege to the capital. [43] The hooves of the Aesir horses pounded like thunder upon the steppes.

[44] Odin himself rode the stoutest of Scythian steeds, Sleipnir, whose speed was such that men drew him with eight legs instead of four. [45] And when the battle came, he cast his spear into the throngs of the Vanir, yet even still they could not overcome their foes. [46] The Vanir rushed forward, trampling the plains on their own steeds, and broke the wall of the Aesir stronghold.
[47] Yet neither side could prevail, and the two peoples made a truce so that they were thenceforth were one nation.

[48] In honor of their peace, they created a potion known as mead, the strength of which was such that it could keep men from battle or compel them to it, depending on how much of it was drunk.

[49] At length, some say that many years after this, a group of them ventured as far as shores of the Baltic Sea, to the place that was to become the realm of Denmark. [50] They remembered the stories of Asgard and Odin, and these they told to their children and their children's children, until the kings and heroes of old became as gods to them.

4

¹ Not all the Danites went north toward the lands of frost and snow. Others among them left their homeland in ships, sailing across the Sea at the Center of the World and beyond, even from the time of Ahmose.

² In those days did some of their number go forth. Among their captains was a certain Nuada, who sailed past the edge of the central sea and ventured beyond the gates to the boundless ocean.

³ This Nuada had ruled over his company for seven years, and at length he brought them to the farthest reaches of the known lands, sailing through the dark mists that conceal the sunrise to make their landing on the northern shores of an emerald isle.

⁴ When they saw this, they were keen to make landing, and they did so at a place called Tracht Mugha in Ulster.

⁵ They brought with them to this place four objects that were as talismans. ⁶ The first of these was the Stone of Fal, which attested to the kingship. The second was the Spear of Lug, which carried the battle. The third was the Sword which was called the Answerer, wielded by Nuada himself. And the forth was the Cauldron of Dagda, from which all men could eat their fill.

⁷ Nuada's people were call themselves the Tuatha De Danaan, which some say refers to the Tribe of Dan and others interpret as People of the Goddess Dana. ⁸ Such was their affection for this fine new land, that they burned their

ships, so there might be no retreat, for they believed they had come upon the land of their ancestors. [9] And indeed, it is said among some that the old gods had fled to the western horizon, as had been told in the tales of Egypt, having grown weary of the ways of men.

[10] Upon their arrival on the shores of the isle that would one day be called Errin, the Tuatha made their way inland a distance to a place called the Red Hills of Rian. [11] There they made their first encampment, and shortly encountered the inhabitants of that place, who were called the Firbolg. [12] These were the "men of bags," who were short of stature and dark of aspect, and who are said to have been the first to play the bagpipes.

[13] The king of that people was one Eochaid Mac Erc, and he sent out from his company a champion named Sreng, armed with two thick spears and a strong shield that was the color of the earth.

[14] And the Tuatha, seeing him come forth, said to themselves, "Behold, a man approaches without any cohort. Surely he means to gather information. Therefore let us send one of our own men to speak with him."

[15] Therefore one named Bres, son of Elatha, went forth from their encampment and strode out toward the one who approached them. [16] Each of them looked the other up and down, taking account of the one who stood before him. For a time, neither man spoke, until at last they deigned to greet one another.

[17] Then Bres entreated Sreng, "Remove your shield from your body and countenance, that I may behold you

and give my fellows an account of your aspect."

[18] And Sreng did so, showing forth his weapons. The points of his javelins were broad, their shafts thick and sturdy. [19] And Bres said, "Woe to the one that should be smitten by them in battle. Woe to him at whom they are flung, against whom they shall be cast, for they are instruments of great torment."

[19] Bres then likewise handed one of his own sharp spears to the other, saying, "Take this as a sample of the weapons the Tuatha wield." [20] And as they drew near to one another, Bres said also, "Give this message to your countrymen: that they must give my people half of your island, or march forth to meet us in battle."

[21] Sreng then answered and said to him, "Truly would I rather part with half our lands than face your weapons in battle." So they made a pact of friendship and went their way.

[22] But when Sreng returned to his people, and he gave them his account of the meeting with Bres, they grew fearful. For he said to them, "Hard it would be to fight them, for their spears are sharp, their shields are strong and their warriors worthy and masterful." [23] Then he told them of the agreement he had made to share the land with the Tuatha, at which they were chagrined, saying, "This we shall not grant, for if we agree, they shall take the whole of the land unto themselves!"

[24] The Tuatha then took counsel among themselves and retreated toward the shores of the sea, saying to themselves, "Let us not stay here, but find a stronghold in

the west; there we shall face whoever might come against us." [25] So they went thence over marsh and plain until they reached a place called Black Hill, where they prepared for whatever might come.

[26] They gathered to themselves seven battalions, who strode out onto the wide field called Magh Nia, which stands near a place between two lakes. And coming to meet them at the opposite side were eleven battalions of the Firbolg.

[27] Their lines stretched forth across the plain, one facing the other, and the Tuatha sent out three among their poets as envoys to King Eochaid, who received them in his tent with gifts at their coming. [28] Yet when they repeated their demand that half the land be ceded to the Tuatha, Eochaid replied, "We shall not grant this request from now to the end of time!"

[29] Both sides therefore agreed to stand down for a short space of time, that they might prepare their weapons for the battle that was to come. [30] In making ready for this day, the Tuatha raised up a fort called the Fort of Onsets, whence they went forth into battle. And the Firbolg entrenched a great fort as their stronghold called the Fort of the Pack, for the packs of dogs that would feast on the bodies of the dead when the battle was over. [31] Each side also made a well of healing filled with herbs where they might tend to the wounds of the fallen.

[32] When they first met on the field of combat, the Firbolg charged fiercely and drove back their enemy, so that they were victorious. [33] Yet they did not pursue the

Tuatha, but returned instead to their own encampment in high spirits at the end of the day.

[34] Even so, the battle was not finished. The champion Dagda fought valiantly for the Tuatha, even slaying the Firbolg warrior Cirb, who before that had sent three hundred men to their deaths. [35] For their part, the Firbolg sent forth Sreng into the melee, and it is said that he slew one hundred and fifty of the Tuatha before reaching Nuada, their king and engaging him in combat. [36] So heavy were the blows of Sreng that, though Nuada turned them aside nine times with his shield, each time was he assailed anew. [37] Then at last Sreng dealt him such a mighty blow that he sliced off the rim of his shield and severed Nuada's right arm at the shoulder.

[38] But before Sreng could deliver a killing blow, two warriors of the Tuatha, Dagda and Aengaba of the North, stood forth between him and the king. [39] Thereupon did Sreng withdraw. And it is said that a hand of silver was fashioned to replace the one Nuada had lost, though he surrendered the kingship on account of his wound.

[40] The Tuatha then made a charge to avenge their king's injury, and they drove deep into the Firbolg company until Bres came face-to-face with the King Eochaid. [41] The king slew him, but Dagda and three other champions of the Tuatha pressed forward to him. [42] That day did many men of the Firbolg die protecting their sovereign.

[43] Then did the Firbolg advance once more against the Tuatha, but their king was weary and stayed behind, charging Sreng and his own son thus: "Continue the fight

while I go in search of a drink, for I can no longer endure this consuming thirst." 44 He therefore withdrew to quench his thirst at the strand called Eothail, nigh unto the seashore. He took with him a hundred men as his guard, but the three sons of Nemed followed him from the Tuatha contingent with a hundred and fifty men. 45 There they surprised Eochaid and his guardsmen, engaging them until all fell and the king along with them.

46 On the field of battle, Eochaid's son fell also, though he in like manner slew the son of Nuada in combat. 47 Such was the fierceness of the blows dealt by one side against the other that, after a day and a night of conflict, each was too weary to lift a hand against the other. So it came about that each side went its own way.

48 And after each side took counsel among its leaders and champions, they came together and made peace. 49 These were the terms: that the Firbolg would retain the land of Connacht, where the battle had been waged and round about it, and that the Tuatha should withdraw to the island's farther regions, all of which would be theirs to rule by treaty.

50 Thence did the Tuatha reign upon the island for nigh unto two hundred years, and their kings were six in number until, at the last, the realm was divided among three chieftains whose signs were the hazel tree, the ploughshare and the blazing sun.

51 But because the land was won by force of arms and price of blood, it was destined to be lost in the same manner. 52 For the sword that rends human flesh also

cleaves asunder peace from justice, shattering one and distorting the other.

5

[1] It was during their reign that Gaythelos and the daughter of Akhenaten set sail out of Egypt in search of a land not touched by the plague. [2] Wind and wave carried them west across the waters until they found a certain watercourse in the land of Numidia, along the north shores of Africa. [3] Making their way upriver in this place, they disembarked there for a time, but could find no rest for themselves there.

[4] Then they betook themselves again to their ships and, as Nuada had done before him, they sailed through the gates to the boundless ocean, remaining near the coastline and following it northward until they found a favorable landing place where they might end their journey.

[5] At this place they removed themselves from their ships and made camp, whereupon they were assailed by the native peoples of that place. [6] Yet Gaythelos and his men prevailed against them and built for themselves a settlement upon a hill close by the ocean. [7] There they built a tower encompassed by a deep ditch, naming the settlement Brigantia, which means "high place," for the hill and the tower that rose above it.

[8] But the people of the land round about Brigantia did continually harry it, until Gaythelos grew weary of warding

them off, for each time he did so, men's lives were lost in the defense of their settlement. [9] He feared that, in time, the people whose land they had invaded would subdue them and subject them to an ignoble life of servitude.

[10] He therefore called upon some of the seamen who had come with him to provision themselves in boats and set out to explore the boundless ocean, beyond any lands that they had known, in the hope of finding a place rich and bountiful that was not yet occupied by any other inhabitant.

[11] Such a place did they indeed discover, then returned to Gaythelos with tidings of its bounty. [12] Now some say that Gaythelos himself espied the land from the top of Brigantia's high tower, yet surely they know now whereof they speak, for the land they found lay far beyond the horizon from that place and was hidden behind the mists that blanket its shores. [13] Indeed, it was the same land to which the Tuatha had come those many years earlier, and this first expedition returned with news of it.

[14] Gaythelos, though, had taken ill and was close to death when the expedition returned. He therefore called his sons to him and said to them, "Whatever may befall me, go forth and make this island your habitation. [15] For in the place where we now dwell, land is difficult to acquire unless it be purchased at far too steep a price, which I fear shall be enslavement and the death of us all. [16] Far better would it be to die bravely in battle than to succumb a little each day beneath the yoke of subjugation."

[17] Therefore he exhorted them, "Go without delay to

the island that is prepared for you, in which place you shall live a life that is noble and free. [18] This is the one gem most sought after by every gentle heart: that is, to endure the sway of no foreign ruler, but to submit freely to the lineage of one's own nation."

[19] Then one of his sons, Ith by name, did go forth on an expedition to the island, taking ninety men with him but leaving his brother behind. [20] They made their landing in the north of the island, near the same spot where the Tuatha had come ashore upon their migration to that place. Indeed, the sons of the Tuatha came out to meet them on a strand called the Fetid Shore.

[21] Ith inquired of them, "What is the name of this place?"

[22] "Inis Elga," said they, which means "Noble Island."

[23] They then took him to a meeting with their kings, who were three in number: Mac Cuill, Mac Cécht and Mac Gréine. [24] Ith came before them and praised their land in their presence, saying, "Good is the land wherein you dwell. [25] Bountiful are its fruits, its honey, its grain and its fish. Temperate is its climate, neither too hot nor too cold. Truly, here you have all that you might need."

[26] But the kings of the Tuatha gleaned from his words that he wished to take possession of the land for himself. Had they not also come and, by force of arms, wrested the island from the Firbolg? [27] They therefore slew one man among Ith's company and bade him to be gone from Inis Elga. [28] Yet when he returned to his ship where he had left them at the Fetid Shore, they fell upon Ith and killed him

as well.

²⁹ After this, some of the men who had come with him retrieved his body and fled the island. Then did they return whence they had come, bringing tidings of what had befallen them and how the inhabitants of Inis Elga had slain their captain. ³⁰ It was for this reason that the Brigantians took to their ships and set out for the island anew, vowing to avenge their prince who had been slain.

³¹ These went out from the coast of Iberia in thirty-six ships, led by one remembered as Milesius, which means "Soldier of Spain." ³² He took with him eight sons and nine brothers, each them determined that they should fulfill Gaythelos' dying wish and build a new settlement on the island they had discovered. ³³ They took with them also the wife of Gaythelos, the princess of Egypt whom he had wed, whose name in her own tongue was Merytaten, but whom they now called Scota.

³⁴ With them also went their judge and bard, Amergin Glúingel. And it is said that when he set foot on the shores of the new land, he spoke thusly:

³⁵ I am wind on sea.
I am ocean wave.
I am roar of sea.
I am bull of seven fights.

³⁶ I am vulture on cliff.
I am dewdrop.
I am fairest of flowers.

I am boar steadfast.

[37] I am salmon in pool.
I am lake on plain.
I am a mountain in a man.
I am a word of skill.

[38] I am the point of a weapon sent forth in combat.
I am god who fashions fire for a head.

[39] Who makes the jagged mountain smooth?
Who is he who proclaims the ages of the moon?
And who, the place where the sun falls in setting?

[40] Then, three days from their arrival did they break camp and do battle with the Tuatha. [41] It was then that Scota, the daughter of the pharaoh, fell in battle. But the Milesians were not to be denied, and they fought fiercely until they had subdued the Tuatha, who from that time forward were seen no more in all the land.

[42] Their abode became the cairns and burial mounds to which they were consigned by the Milesian invaders, and their names became echoes from a distant past. [43] The Tribe of Dan was no more in the land of Inis Elga, their memories obscured beyond the mists of time, relegated to the land of legend.

[44] Thenceforth, for many years, the island's name was changed to Scota, in honor of the fallen queen of Egypt who never sat upon the throne of that land but who, in her

death, became the queen of a new country. ⁴⁵ And in the time ahead, many of her people crossed the narrow straight to another island, which land also took her name as its own, whereas in that day the people took to calling Inis Elga, Errin.

6

¹ Not all the Danites perished on that western isle. Many remained in their ships. Indeed, they grew mighty and their ships subdued the world. ² Their captains traded with Tarshish in Iberia, which belonged to Hiram, king of Tyre, whose own city gave this distant port its name. ³ They traded in gold and silver, in bronze, in tin and copper, and thus did they magnify both their name and their fortune.

⁴ They rose up from the waters as a great storm, which was born in the Sea at the Center of the World, and moved across the waters in strength and boldness. ⁵ The Warriors of the Great Green Sea, they called them, and the people of the Phoenix they were. ⁶ Such was their strength in arms that no land could stand before them. The empire of the Hittites, which had withstood the armies of Egypt's pharaohs, was laid waste at their landing.

⁷ They were many in number, and no man knew their homeland, for they were from everywhere and nowhere. As ghosts they sailed the central sea, raiding the coastal lowlands and watching all nations submit before them. ⁸ In confidence did they advance on Ugarit, along the seacoast

in the land of Syria. And the king of that nation cried out in terror at their arrival. He pleaded for help from those who were his allies. To the king of Cyprus he sent this letter:

[9] "Behold! The enemy's ships have come. My cities are burned, and the country is beset by evils. [10] Do you not know, my father, that my foot soldiers and chariots are in the land of the Hittites, and all my ships are abroad in Lydia? [11] Thus my land is abandoned to itself. Let it be known, my father, that seven ships from the enemy have inflicted great hardship upon us."

[12] Yet he found no help from that quarter.

[13] And he sent forth also a missive to the king of Carchemish, whose land was to the north by the mighty Euphrates. Yet from Carchemish also, no more than sage advice was sent in answer:

[14] "As for what you have written me, 'Ships of the enemy have been seen at sea!,' you must remain steadfast," came the answer. [15] "Where are your troops and chariots stationed? Are they not close by you? Or if not, then behind the enemy that assails you? [16] Therefore surround your towns with ramparts. There you must await the enemy with your chariots and foot soldiers at the ready. Stand fast with great resolve!"

[17] Yet the kingdom of Ugarit could not stand fast. The enemy poured in upon them like seawater through an open floodgate. And in a moment, the nation was no more.

[18] The peoples of the sea came from everywhere, as if from nowhere. They swept like spirits across the waves from Italy in the land of the Etruscans. [19] From Achaea, the

land of the Greeks. From Sardinia and Sicily. And from the northern coast of Canaan, from the five cities of the Philistines. [20] It was there, in the land of Philistia, that they encountered the armies of the Elohim, and it was there that the land was rent asunder in bloody warfare between the servants of Yahweh and the masters of the sea, the people of Dan.

[21] First, however, the seafarers set their sights on the grandest prize of all, on Egypt, the empire of the pharaohs. [22] In the days of the Pharaoh Merenptah, they brought their ships to ground on the coast of the Nile Delta. There did they combine their men and weapons with those from the tribes of Libya, finding common cause with them against the empire of Egypt. [23] Together, they formed a fighting force of sixteen thousand men, marching inland to Memphis and also Heliopolis.

[24] Yet Merenptah repulsed them, killing six thousand of their number and routing the remainder of their forces.

[25] Even still they took courage. And in the eighth year of Merenptah's successor, Rameses, they made haste to renew their assault on Egypt. [26] Yet Rameses, the third pharaoh to bear that name, strengthened his forces in the south of Canaan and fortified the many mouths of the Nile. [27] The archers of Rameses struck down the seafarers before they could reach the shores of Egypt. [28] They lay in ambush in the mouths of the mighty Nile, in the marshes of the Delta. [29] They sent forth their arrows like a plague of stinging locusts, and their ships emerged from hiding amid the reeds and rushes of the lowland. [30] Then did the pharaoh's navy

ensnare the ships of their enemies, the seafarers, using the barbs of their grappling hooks. And after this they pulled the vessels of woe aground in the marshland of the Delta.

[31] There did the foot soldiers of Egypt assail them, until the invaders were turned back and utterly vanquished.

[32] "As for those who came forth to my borders, their seed has vanished. Their hearts and souls are crushed for all eternity. [33] Those who went forth upon the sea sailed into the heart of a flame fully kindled. [34] At the mouths of our great river did we meet them. And a stronghold of lances surrounded them upon the shore."

[35] Thus did Rameses boast of his victory, yet the seafarers were not defeated. [36] To the southern coast of Canaan they withdrew, finding refuge in their five coastal cities: Ashkelon and Ekron, Ashdod and Gaza, and Gath, the home of the Gittites.

[37] The coast of Asia was their domain as well. There they dwelt in a city beside Mount Ida, a city known as Troy.

7

[1] The city of Troy grew from the mists of time and memory, seated upon the eastern coast of Asia. The ancients say it was founded by one Ilus, son of Tros, who named it for his father. Yet others still called it Ilium, after him.

[2] Its place near the mouth of a narrow strait gave it mastery of the passageway between the Sea at the Center of the World and, to the north and east, the Dark Sea. [3] In like

manner, it stood as sentinel along the land road from Asia into Europe. [4] As guardian of these two great passageways, over land and on the waves, the people of Troy amassed a great fortune exacting tolls from ships and caravans.

[5] For their own part, the Trojans built an ample fleet in which they sailed forth with their allies, the same seafarers who assailed Egypt and the Hittites. [6] And the nations round about chafed beneath the yoke of the Trojans, saying to themselves, "It is madness that we allow this to continue! See how they rob us as we pass beside the isthmus! And they use the tolls they impose upon our travelers to build yet more ships for their navy!"

[7] Such was the wealth of the Trojans that King Priam, who led them, sired fifty sons and a dozen daughters by his wife and many concubines.

[8] And the tale is told that his son Paris was invited to serve as judge in the pavilion of Olympus. There, in the city of the gods, it fell upon him to choose who was the fairest. [9] The one so favored would receive in token of her triumph a single golden apple, inscribed with the words "For the most beautiful." [10] Yet which among them would it be? Would the honor fall to Athena, the guardian of Athens? Or to Hera, the consort of mighty Zeus? Or to Aphrodite, the foam-born maiden? [11] Whichever choice he made, Paris would surely incur the wrath of two great goddesses, while earning gratitude from only one.

[12] His mind, it is said, was made up by an overture from Aphrodite, who promised that he should win the heart of the world's most beautiful woman should he decide the

matter in her favor. [13] That woman, however, belonged to another man, Menelaus, king of Sparta.

[14] So it was that Paris set sail for Sparta under the guise of diplomacy to make off with Helen, as Aphrodite had promised. It is written that he succeeded, and that the Spartans, in league with their allies from Achaea, made haste to retrieve her.

[15] Yet is not Helen the name by which the Achaeans call their own people? Are they not Hellenes, and is their land not Hellas? [16] Indeed, it was no woman that the Trojans had stolen, but the wealth of Achaea itself. [17] By deception and diplomacy, through their sea tolls and taxes, they had made off with the wealth of Achaea; they had plundered her without bloodshed.

[18] As it is the wont of men to blame the gods for their ambitions, to attribute to the heavens their own folly, so it was in this case.

[19] It therefore came to pass that the Achaeans, weary of the Trojan tariffs, gathered an armada to recover the whole of their losses. [20] And they set sail across the Aegean to face the Trojans in a war that lasted one year, two years, five years, ten years, until both sides despaired that it should ever be concluded.

As it is written,

[21] The sun of a new day struck the ploughlands,
Rising up from the quiet water
And the deep stream of the ocean
To climb the sky.

²² Then did the Trojans assemble together.
But they could scarce recognize each one fallen,
So with the water washed away the blood upon them,
And wept warm tears as they bore them to the wagons.

²³ But great Priam, their king, forbade them mourn
aloud.
So in silence did they pile their bodies on the pyre,
Their hearts vexed with sorrow,
And did burn them on the fire,
Then returned to sacred Ilium

²⁴ In like manner did the Achaeans, sorely grieved,
Pile the slain among their number on the pyre,
Their hearts vexed with sorrow,
And did burn them on the fire,
Then returned to their hollow vessels

²⁵ The Greeks went forth and, in their fighting,
desecrated temples of the Trojans around about the city,
among them the sanctuary of Athena. Yet still, they could
not prevail. ²⁶ At last, the Achaeans feigned withdrawal,
pulling their ships back from the coastline and leaving in
their wake a single gift: a horse whose hide and mane were
wood, and whose legs were borne by wheels. ²⁷ Planks of
fur they wove across its ribs. Three days it took them to
build it, and its size was like unto a mountain. ²⁸ And when
it was completed the Greeks said, "Hearken to our words,

you Trojans. Athena has tasked us to build her this great beast as a gift for you, to atone for our desecration of her temple in your city."

[29] But Laocoon, a priest of Troy, counseled them strenuously, saying, "Do you truly think the enemy departed? That he has sailed away upon the foamy seas? Do you truly judge that any Greek gift be free of treachery? Is this the reputation of their leader, Odysseus? [30] Nay, either the Achaeans are in hiding, concealed by the wood of this breathless beast, or they have conceived it as a mechanism to use against our walls. Or to spy upon our homes. Or to fall upon us from above. [31] Perhaps then also, it conceals some other deceit. Trust not this horse, my fellow Trojans. Whatever it may be, I fear the Greeks, even bearing gifts."

[32] And he let fly his spear with a mighty hand, so that it pierced the side of the creature with great force. It struck there, quivering, so that the cavity within rang hollow. And there was heard in that place a mighty groan.

[33] Yet the Trojans heeded not his warnings, and they took the horse into the city. In its belly were hidden thirty soldiers, and in its mouth two Achaean spies. [34] So it came to pass, after nightfall, that the ships of Greece sailed back toward the city. [35] And as the Trojans slept inside their homes, the Achaeans crept forth from the belly of the beast, and they opened the gates for their countrymen, who flooded the city with their numbers. [36] Thus was the siege of Troy ended at last, and the Trojans defeated in a rout by means of subterfuge.

[37] But the Trojans were not all slain in the battle. Aeneas, a cousin to the king, escaped, it is said, to the country of Latium, whence come the tribe of the Latins who are mighty to this day. [38] Two of his descendants, some say, founded the city of Rome. And one among his grandsons is claimed as the founder of a line of kings in Britain.

8

[1] Aphrodite was the patron goddess of all the seafaring peoples. [2] As the foam-born did she guide them to safety on the waves. From her perch in the starry heavens did she light a beacon for them to follow, the brightest in the evening sky. [3] In the form of a dove had she guided Noah to safe landing. The softness of her wings bespoke of love and inspiration, and oft did she descend upon the tongues of bards and sages.

[4] The Greeks did name her Aphrodite, but the seafarers knew her as Astarte. She was favored of the Trojans and, in like manner, of the Philistines, who dwelt upon the southern coast of Canaan. [5] From their cities did they launch their many ships of trade and plunder. Yet also were their foot soldiers and chariots at the ready. [6] And the armies of the Elohim did challenge them, but they did answer, and it came to pass that the Danites of Philistia lorded it over the Elohim and their followers, such that they chafed at beneath their yoke.

[7] In that place, in those days, many strong men had

arisen. The men did call them giants, for great was their brutality and vast was their ambition. [8] Yet their reach extended beyond their grasp, and their vanity exceeded the truth of things. [9] Kings they were not, but petty princes and pretenders, tyrants and usurpers. Each ruled a plot of land that was little more than a collection of fields and threshing floors, brought together by their conquests of nearby farms and pasture.

[10] They boasted, "I am the king of Moab!" Or of Ammon. Or of Edom. Or of Judah. And they conscripted men to battle, waging war on one another in the manner of great empires.

[11] Yet no empires were these. To Egypt, they were but gnats to be swatted; to Babylon, they were but vassals to be yoked. [12] So did Merneptah, who turned the seafarers back from Egypt, proclaim of them: "Canaan is captive to all woe. Ashekelon is conquered, Gezer seized, Yanoam banished from all existence. Israel is laid waste, barren of seed."

[13] Ashkelon was a city of the Philistines. And another of these cities was Timnah.

[14] To Timnah came the champion of the Danites, whose name was Samson. His land of birth was a short distance away, at the edge of the land called Judah. No king was he, but a man of war who sought to secure for himself a place of power. [15] For this purpose did he seek alliance with the chief man of Timnah through marriage to his daughter.

[16] He said to his father and mother, "I would have her, for she pleases me." And they sought to dissuade him, yet

he would not accept their answer. ¹⁷ At length, therefore, he set out from his home town toward Timnah, which was but an hour's walk distant. ¹⁸ And when he had come to the vineyards that belonged to that place, it is said that he came upon a fierce young lion, which set upon him. ¹⁹ He therefore rose up and slew the whelp, rending its flesh in two with his own bare hands.

²⁰ Yet surely this did not occur. For is it not written, "Dan is a lion's whelp?" And likewise also, the same is said of Judah. ²¹ So it was that Samson, who was born at the border between these two tribes, would rend both of them in two for the sake of his ambition. And it happened in the following manner.

²² When Samson arrived at the Timnah, the chief man of the village agreed to his proposal to forge an alliance, and a feast was prepared according to the custom. ²³ Then the father of the man appointed to Samson thirty companions, for he said to himself, "If this man plots against me, these shall hear of it and slay him."

²⁴ But Samson knew this, and so did challenge them: "Come and answer me this riddle. If you declare to me the answer in seven days, I shall bestow upon you thirty linen garments and thirty sets of clothes. But if you fail in this charge, you must provide me the same."

²⁵ Then the thirty asked him to speak his riddle. And he said, "From the eater came forth meat, and from the strong came sweetness."

²⁶ But they could not answer him after three days. After four days, they had no reply. After five days, they were

speechless. After six days, their tongues were silent. [27] And on the seventh day, they went forth to their kinswoman, whom Samson had taken as his wife, and besought her, saying, "Entice your husband, that he may explain to you this riddle. Then speak the answer to us, that we may preserve your household."

[28] The woman therefore went to Samson, entreating and accusing him: "Your hatred burns against me! Your love is false! For you have asked my people this riddle, yet kept from me its answer."

[29] He sought at first to forestall her, for he had not told even his own parents the answer. Yet she persisted, so that at the last he relented and told her. [30] Then at once did she go to her people and say to them, "This is the answer to the riddle: What is sweeter than honey? And what is stronger than a lion?"

[31] So when the time came, before the sun set on the seventh day, the men of the town approached Samson and gave him the answer his wife had told them. [32] And Samson was wroth with fury, for his own deception was turned against him. [33] He therefore cursed and said to them, "Had you not plowed with my heifer, you would ne'er have solved my riddle!"

[34] And in his anger, he went forth to Ashkelon and there struck down thirty men of the Philistines in that city. He stripped them of their garments and cast them in a heap at the feet of those who had solved the riddle. [35] So did he shed innocent blood in vengeance for his wife's deception. [36] Then he went forth from that place to the home of his

kinsmen, but his wife had been removed from his presence and given to one of the thirty from the feast. Her father would not allow him to go in to her, saying, "She is given to another. Take her younger sister instead."

[37] Samson, however, was greatly offended, for he who had taken the eldest sister now had first claim upon her father's estate. And Samson said to himself, "If I cannot advance my purpose by guile, I shall turn Timnah an Ashkelon against one another!"

[38] Then, going out, he caught three hundred foxes and tied torches to their tails, whereupon he released them into the fields. [39] These ran in terror through the stalks of grain, lighting it afire so that all the land was ablaze. [40] And the beasts themselves were set afire, and were consumed along with the grain. Their cries did rise to the heavens, born upon their deathly anguish. [41] Some say the gods did hear them, and remembered the evil done by Samson, and turned from him. But others scorn him not only for this, but also for his murder of the Philistines.

[42] Even so, when the burned fields were discovered, the blame was placed on the man of Timnah, who had withheld his daughter from Samson. [43] So his countrymen from among the Philistines set upon both the woman and her father, and burned them to death, in the same way that their fields had been burned. [44] In this way did Samson accomplish his purpose, setting Philistine against Philistine because of his anger.

9

¹ Yet still Samson's ire was not assuaged, and he said to himself, "Even now I am denied that which is due to me, so I shall surely slay the ones responsible with my own two hands!"

² And madness took him, as is wont to happen in the hearts of men who are bent on vengeance. ³ He saw no farther than the point of his sword and no deeper than the depth of his fury. And he went forth to slaughter them, saying, "I will not stop until I have my vengeance!"

⁴ When, therefore, he had spilled the blood of many a man, he retreated to a high cave in the hill country of Judah, the rock of an eyrie, which is called Etam, where he hid himself. ⁵ For though the madness was upon him, he knew that vengeance begets vengeance, and in due course the kinsmen of those he had assaulted would go forth seeking retribution.

⁶ So indeed they did. They went forth against the land of Judah, the land of the Elohim, because this is where Samson had hid himself. ⁷ They spread their forces out, pitching their camp near Lehi to the south of Jerusalem.

⁸ Then the Judahites came out to meet the Philistines and questioned them, saying, "Wherefore have you come forth to fight us?"

⁹ "We have come for Samson, to take him captive," they said. "We would do to him as he has done to us."

¹⁰ So the Judahites rode out to the cave at Etam and laid hold of Samson, binding him hand and foot, for he was not

of their tribe and they wished no part of him.

[11] They took him from that place to meet the Philistines. But as they approached the encampment at Lehi, Samson loosed the bonds that held him, so they dropped like flax that had burned in a fire. [12] And the tale is told that he picked up the jawbone of an ass that lay in the field there, and that with this weapon he slew a thousand men.

[13] After these things, the men of Judah feared Samson, wherefore he held sway over them and did as he pleased. But the Philistines of Timnah and Ashkelon were ever at his heels. Yet still did he spend many days among them, for he was, like them, a Danite.

[14] One day, he went in to a harlot in Gaza, and his enemies lay in wait for him, surrounding that place, yet he escaped them. [15] And he found there a woman of that country named Delilah, and he desired her. The woman's home was in the Valley of Sorek. (This is the valley where Timnah was found, the home of Samson's wife in his youth.)

[16] Now Samson took Delilah to himself, but his enemies besought her, saying, "Discover the source of Samson's might, that we may subdue him."

[17] So she shaved his head as he was sleeping, that he might become a mockery. And the men of Gaza came in to him as he lay with her and bound him with fetters of brass. [18] They put out his eyes and confined him. And they presented him to their god Dagon, the lord of fishermen and ploughmen, saying, "Here is the bane of the Philistines, brought low by our great nation."

¹⁹ Yet the gods saw these things and remarked among themselves, "How long shall this continue? Vengeance begets vengeance, and strife begets strife. And always it continues, lest at length we put a stop to it."

²⁰ It therefore came to pass that the men of Gaza gathered for their feast day, and they tied Samson between two pillars. And they made sport of him. ²¹ But there came a mighty rumbling from beneath the earth, so that the pillars shook and trembled. ²² Some then said, "It is Samson! He moves the pillars!" Yet others said, "The gods are wroth with us, and the earth shall swallow us alive!"

²³ The walls did crack, and the pillars did buckle, and the stones that had been laid one on top of the other were loosened. ²⁴ Then did the walls come down in a torrent of dust and rubble, like a wave from the sea crashing hard against the shoreline. ²⁵ They fell upon blind Samson. They fell upon the men of Gaza. They fell upon all who assembled in that place. ²⁶ And so were their iniquities revisited on all of them.

²⁷ Yet the folly of man was not so easily ended, nor his thirst for conflict so swiftly quenched. ²⁸ Therefore did the death of mad Samson bring no end to the cycle of violence, and the Judahites made war anew upon the Danites of Philistia, and the Danites upon the Judahites. And the gods turned away in revulsion.

²⁹ And the wheel of time moved forward. The ages passed on from days of bronze, and weapons of iron fired in forges of blackest intent were made ready for great battles. ³⁰ They drew the blood of men and rent the hearts

of women. Children died without mercy. The land was laid waste.

[31] And the gods wept.

The Book of

Contendings

1

¹ These are the chronicles of the land of Judah and Israel during the time of their first princes, the record of their reigns and the violence done in the name of the gods.

² This is how the city of Zion rose to the heights of pride and vanity on the shoulders of the vanquished, how the Elohim spread strife across the land of Canaan and how the scions of Avaris contended with the people of the

Phoenix.

³ In those days, the children of Shem found no rest for themselves. Their time on earth was short, and ever were they afflicted. ⁴ On one side, the priests of the Elohim oppressed them. On the other, the nations round about assailed them. ⁵ They would rise up against the Elohim in the cause of freedom. Yet then would the nations of Ammon and Moab and Edom come against them. Then would the Philistines besiege them.

⁶ Then, having no man as a bulwark against those who would subdue them, they would cry out. They would appeal to the Elohim once more, saying, "Save us!"

⁷ So it was that the people came to seek, in their affliction, a deliverer. ⁸ Looking not to themselves for salvation, they sought instead a champion. Seeking not to guard their own freedom, they placed this charge in the hands of another. ⁹ Then would the Elohim appoint a judge to lead them, a priest and prophet whose hand was heavy. ¹⁰ In strength would he subdue the enemy, and in strength would he restrain his own people, until such time as they should rebel once more.

¹¹ In those days, the judges dwelt in Shiloh, and they passed judgment upon the people. ¹² Such a one was Eli, whose name means "ascended one of El," for he bore the ancient title of Most High. ¹³ Beside him served his two sons, Hophni and Phinehas. But their edicts were unjust, and they reeked with the stench of corruption. ¹⁴ They would take to their loins the women who served at the tent of meeting. They would demand sacrifices for their

polluted altars, and partake of the best meat themselves.
[15] Plunging the fleshhook into the cauldron, they would take up for themselves the choicest portions. And if any dared resist, they would say, "We shall have it, then, by force." This was the way of the House of Eli.

[16] Now in the course of time, Eli grew old and weary, and his sight had begun to fail. He therefore appointed for himself a servant, who might minister to him in all things. [17] He chose a tester of winds and a reader of portents, who might report to Eli all that transpired throughout the land. For this reason, Eli called him Samuel, which means "the ears of Eli."

[18] But when Eli had grown yet more feeble, Samuel took counsel with himself, saying, "The one I serve will soon be dead, and the people abide not the ways of his sons. They shall surely rise up against Hophni and Phinehas. And then will I not be slain as well? [19] Therefore shall I arise and take the mantle of Eli to myself. In this way shall I become Most High, and gain renown the savior of the people."

[20] So did he contrive within his heart. He lay in wait, until he was alone with Eli and no one was there to defend the old man. Then did he enter his chamber and say to him: "I have heard the word of Yahweh."

[21] And Eli said, "Speak. Withhold it not from me."

[22] Then did Samuel say to him, "Behold! I shall accomplish something that will cause the ears of all who hear to tingle! I shall visit upon Eli what he has visited on his people. [23] I shall judge his house for all eternity because he knew of its corruption, yet did nothing to restrain it. He

knew of his sons' perversions, yet did nothing to deny them. ²⁴ Therefore I swear now before all the nation: My wrath upon the House of Eli shall never be assuaged. ²⁵ No atonement shall be made for his corruption, neither by sacrifice nor by offerings on the altar. For this altar has been polluted by the wicked, and the land has been laid waste for their injustice!"

²⁶ Eli's eyes then flashed with anger, though they were milky white from blindness. And he cursed Samuel and spat from his dry and aged lips, "If this is the word of Yahweh, let him do what is right in his own eyes!"

²⁷ And he called his sons to him and warned them of all that Samuel intended. But Samuel caused the words that he himself had spoken to be heard throughout the land, and many among the people believed them, for they scorned the House of Eli.

²⁸ Hophni and Phinehas therefore said to themselves, "Come now! We shall raise an army against the Philistines and assail them. When therefore we prevail and make them our servants, we shall subdue the land once more. ²⁹ Then shall the people hail us anew as their anointed ones. And then shall Samuel perish!"

³⁰ So it came to pass that the sons of Eli the judge rode out against the Philistines. And they brought with them the ark of the covenant. ³¹ This was the ark fashioned by the Elohim as a symbol of their power and dominion. And some among the Philistines were vexed at the sight of it, saying, "A god has come into the midst of them. For this reason, we shall surely fail. ³² Are these not the gods of the

Egyptians, who defeated us in Ashkelon? Is this not the ark of slain Osiris? Behold, the wings of the two goddesses who guard it!"

³³ Upon seeing it, some among them counseled withdrawal. ³⁴ But others prevailed upon them saying, "Have courage, lest these people make us their subjects, even as they themselves have been subject to us! Take courage, therefore, and fight!"

³⁵ And the Philistines went forth from that place and defeated their enemies, showing them no quarter. ³⁶ Each man from the camp of the Elohim fled in terror, abandoning their tents and forsaking their companions. ³⁷ Thousands of soldiers died that day. And the Philistines slew the sons of Eli, and they captured the ark from the encampment.

³⁸ At this did the Shemites gasp in wonder. They stood as mute children in the face of a mighty storm. They watched with eyes open, yet disbelieving. ³⁹ And when Eli himself was brought news of it, it is said that he fell backward from the place where he was sitting so that his neck was broken. ⁴⁰ Yet others say that he was murdered; some say by a Philistine, and others by the will of Samuel, at the hand of his own people who now scorned him.

⁴¹ Some among them despised the ark itself. For they said, "This is not the true ark that was crafted by the ancients! Were it so, this would not have befallen us!"

⁴² And others said, "Behold, now all is lost to us!"

⁴³ The Philistines took the ark to Ashdod, and they showed it to the people. ⁴⁴ They paraded it through their

cities as a sign of their triumph. In Gath and in Ekron they displayed it as a testament to their greatness. [45] Yet the people were afraid, thinking the pharaoh would come to reclaim it, or that the gods might be wroth with them for taking it. [46] (For upon seeing it, many thought it the true ark of Osiris, the one to whom their own master Dagon had bowed before the armies of Merneptah). [47] And some said, "This ark is as a plague to us!"

[48] So they removed it from their presence and returned it to the precincts near Jerusalem. [49] And they went back again to their own people, saying, "See? No harm or plague has come upon us! The ark is but an empty vessel, as the boasts of Eli were empty threats! [50] Is there a plague among us? Nay, but the gold we have taken from the armies of our enemies shall be crafted in the likeness of tumors, and it shall take the form of rats. Thus shall we mock our enemies and their false god!"

[51] Samuel therefore received the ark back from them with a delegation from Shiloh and Jerusalem, and in that day took credit for its return. [52] He told then people, "See how Dagon, the god of the Philistines, has bowed at the feet of Yahweh? For the ark became a plague upon them, and they have restored it to our people!"

[53] But some of the men who were with him had heard the Philistines boasting. And when the Philistines had departed, they opened the ark and looked inside it, so that the truth of the matter became known to them. [54] For this reason did the Samuel order each of them put to death, seventy in all, that they might be silenced and the nation

might not be told of their deception. [55] And after this, they removed the ark from their presence and sent it away to Kiriath-Jearim, which is the city of the woods, to the east of Jerusalem. There it remained for twenty years.

[56] And the people demanded a new champion, an anointed one they called "messiah." (Now messiah, in their tongue, means anointed one.) [57] And they bestowed this honor on Samuel, who had sought it with his scheming. Then did he rise up to lead their armies against the Philistines.

2

[1] But the House of Samuel followed the ways of the House of Eli, becoming fat and wealthy from the labors of the people. [2] The sons of Samuel, whom he anointed, accepted bribes and issued false decrees. They piled abuse upon abuse. They heaped injustice on injustice. [3] So now the people grew restless and weary of their lot, and they cried out, saying, "Behold! The Philistines are far from us, yet the House of Samuel is near at hand, inflicting woes more grievous than the blows of any army!"

[3] Therefore they demanded of Samuel, "Give us a king, after the manner of other nations, that he may lead us."

[4] But Samuel wished to preserve the station he had gained for himself, and so protested. [5] He said to the people: "This is what a king will do should he reign over you. He will make your sons serve you with his chariots

and horses, and they shall run before your horses. [6] Some he will assign as commanders of thousands and fifties. Others he will cause to plow his ground and reap his harvests. Others still will make weapons for his wars, or will help equip his chariots.

[7] "Your daughters he shall take to be his confectionaries, cooks and bakers. [8] He will take your vineyards from you, and your fields and olive gardens, and he will give them to his favorites — his officers and servants. [9] He shall afflict your men and maidservants with labor, and he shall use your asses for his own purpose. [10] A tenth of your sheep he shall take from you. And you shall be his servants."

[11] Yet the people heeded not this warning. Did not the House of Samuel call their sons to service? Had not many of these words found fruition already by the old priest's actions?

[12] It therefore came to pass that Samuel feared the people might rise against him, as they had done in the days of Eli. [13] So he took counsel with himself and said, "I shall choose for this nation a king beholden to my word, who relies upon my counsel and dares not act without my sanction."

[14] And he anointed for the people a man from the tribe of Benjamin, the smallest and the weakest among all the clans of Canaan. [15] This man was called by the name of Saul. He was great in stature and fair to behold, yet in truth he was as feeble as a foal made lame from its mother's womb. [16] At the coming of Samuel to his village, even he himself protested, saying, "Am I not a Benjamite? Is my

clan not the least, without significance? Wherefore should I be chosen to lead the people?"

[17] But Samuel hearkened not to these words, and proceeded according to his purpose. So did he present Saul to the people, to all the sons of Israel, saying, "Behold the king who shall rule over you!"

[18] And Saul did everything that Samuel instructed him, for he had not the means to challenge him. [19] Straightaway, after his anointing, he led the armies of Israel against the Ammonites, who had laid siege to Jabesh in Gilead. [20] And the king of Ammon refused their entreaties, saying, "I will withdraw this siege on a single condition: that you remove the right eye of every man among you, and in doing so bring disgrace upon all of Israel!"

[21] When he heard this, Saul burned hot with anger. And he took two oxen and hacked them to pieces at the point of his own sword. [22] Then did he send messengers to all of Israel. With them, he sent the meat of the oxen, covered in flies and stained bright red from the flow of its blood. [23] And he gave them this message to proclaim: "Such shall be the fate of any man who opposes Saul and Samuel!" [24] So did he seek to procure by threat the loyalty of men, which he could not win through honor.

[25] Then did he assemble an army and make haste to Jabesh in Gilead. And he feigned to the king of Ammon that he would surrender. But he did not.

[26] He divided his men into three divisions, and he had them lie in wait until the sunset. [27] Then did he assail the camp of Ammon as the night fell, and he slaughtered them

from eventide to the heat of the following day. Those not slain were put to flight, until no two men were left standing together. ²⁸ Then did the men of Israel hail him, saying, "Truly Saul is a worthy king, and mighty!" And they gave him their allegiance that very day, along with the men of Jabesh whom he had rescued.

²⁹ But Samuel they credited not with the victory. And Saul alone won their praises.

3

¹ Now Samuel began to regret that he had anointed Saul as king, for he had grown mighty in his own right and beloved of his subjects. Yet Israel despised the name of Samuel for the sake his corruption and because he lorded it over the people.

² Samuel therefore assembled the people and said to them, "I have done as you asked of me and anointed a king to rule you. I am old, and the hairs on my head are gray as ashes. My sons are here among you, and I have led you from my youth until this very day. ³ So bring your charge against me. Whose ox have I taken, and whom have I defrauded? Whose donkey have I stolen, and whom have I oppressed? From whose hand have I accepted bribes, that I might shut my eyes to justice? ⁴ If I have done any of these things, I shall provide recompense. I swear it."

⁵ But the people said nothing, for they feared Saul and his armies. Had not Samuel anointed him? And had not Saul himself carved up the ox flesh, saying, "Such shall be

the fate of any man who opposes Saul and Samuel"?

[6] In fear, yet not in truth, they answered, "You have defrauded no man among us, neither have you oppressed us. Nor have you stolen anything from the hand of any person."

[7] Samuel therefore said to them, "Yahweh is therefore my witness against you!"

[8] And he turned to Saul, who stood beside him, and said, "Here is the king you have chosen, the one you asked for! See? [9] Yahweh has given you a king to rule you. Do you think for this reason you can curse the name of Yahweh? That you can turn aside from his precepts and forsake the commands of the Most High? [10] But no! If you fear Yahweh and keep his commands, if you and the king who rules over you does not stray from him, then it will be well with you. [11] But if you should rebel against Yahweh, his hand will be against you, even as it was also against your forebears!

[12] "Now raise your eyes and behold what Yahweh shall do in your sight this day. Is the wheat harvest not upon you? [13] Therefore, I shall call upon Yahweh to bring forth rain and thunder from the heavens. Perhaps then it shall be plain the depth of this foul deed you have done in asking for a king to rule over you!

[14] "As for me, far be it from me that I might defy Yahweh and neglect to pray for you! [15] I shall instruct you in what is good and proper. Yet if you persist in doing evil, you shall perish — and your king along with you!"

[16] When Saul heard these things, he began to consider

them. He pondered their import and questioned their truth.
[17] And it grew clear in his mind that Samuel's intent was to
betray him; that he had been chosen for the priest's own
purpose, to be discarded at the proper time. [18] When
Samuel had suppressed the enmity that had risen against
him, he would use some pretext to cast aside his lackey and
assume the mantle of leadership anew. [19] This he would
pass to his sons in the proper time; in this manner would
the seed of corruption be sewn anew in Israel. As their
king, he could not abide this.

[20] Saul therefore rose up against Philistines and the
other nations round about them. He smote the Philistine
garrison at Geba, and he amassed an army of men to send
forth against the enemy, for he sought to win the loyalty of
the people through a show of force.

[21] Samuel therefore said to him, "Go ahead of me to
Gilgal. I will surely come down to you and sacrifice burnt
offerings and offerings of fellowship. [22] But you must tarry
seven days there and do nothing until I arrive there to
instruct you!"

[23] He said this knowing that the Philistines would arrive
before the appointed time, and that Saul dared not
command the army without the needed offerings. [24] When,
therefore, Samuel failed to arrive as promised, Saul's men
would be put to flight and his name would be uttered only
in contempt.

[25] When Saul therefore did as he was bidden, this is
what occurred at Gilgal. [26] The Philistines assembled there
chariots beyond number with their charioteers. They

gathered fighting men to that place, more numerous than the sands of the seashore. [27] These went up and pitched camp at Michmash, and the men of Israel saw it. Then did they hide themselves in caves and thickets, among the rocks, in pits and cisterns. [28] Some even began to leave the field, fleeing beyond the Jordan to Gad and Gilead.

[29] Yet still Saul waited. And when the seven days had passed, the rest of men began to scatter, saying, "This man is not fit to lead us! His army deserts him before his eyes, yet he waits for that cur Samuel's sanction!"

[30] And Saul knew he had been abandoned.

[31] He therefore commanded his generals, "Bring the burnt offering to me, and the fellowship offerings with it!" And the men rallied to him, seeing now his strength of purpose.

[32] But when Samuel arrived, he cursed him, saying, "What is this thing you have done? Sacrifice is a priestly duty, entrusted to the Most High. Do you dare challenge the one who made you king, when such is my right alone?"

[33] Saul therefore answered and said to him, "The men began to scatter, and you were not steadfast in your word to me. The Philistine army was poised to slaughter us at Gilgal, and I had not made the proper sacrifice.

[34] "What trick is this you have fashioned to ensnare me? If I made no sacrifice, the blood would have been upon your hands for your deception. Yet now you dare upbraid me for failing to keep my end of the bargain? You, who did not keep your part with me? [35] Nay! You are no more than a scheming charlatan, intent upon yoking the people to

your treachery! ³⁶ You anointed a king to serve you, then thought to discard me and sacrifice the men of Israel on your polluted altar. ³⁷ May it never be! I stand now to oppose you. And my armies shall prove the right of it!"

³⁸ Then Saul therefore took six hundred men and departed from that place, together with his son Jonathan, and led his forces east toward the Philistine encampment. ³⁹ And in his fury, he swore an oath, saying, "Cursed be anyone who eats food before evening comes, ere I have avenged myself against my enemies!"

⁴⁰ But his son Jonathan had separated himself from the main company and went now in stealth with his armor bearer to the far side of the enemy camp. Then he said to his armor bearer, "Let us go up to their outpost."

⁴¹ Therefore his armor bearer answered, saying, "Do everything that is in your mind to do. I am with you, heart and soul."

⁴² So they went forward, passing between two sheer cliffs that formed a pass behind the encampment, and Jonathan said to his armor-bearer, "Come, let us cross over toward the enemy that they may catch sight of us. ⁴³ If they set forth against us, we will stand back and not engage them. But if they bid us go forth to them, we shall climb up and fall upon them." ⁴⁴ (He said this because he knew that if they should not come forth willingly, it would be because they were fearful and unprepared.)

⁴⁵ This then is what happened: When the Philistines caught sight of Jonathan and his armor-bearer, they called out to them, saying, "Behold! The Hebrews are crawling

out of the holes in which they have hidden themselves. Come up to us, therefore, and we shall teach you a lesson."

⁴⁶ At this, Jonathan and his armor bearer climbed up high into the cliffs that guarded the pass. And when the Philistines thought they had retreated in fear, they pursued them. ⁴⁷ It was then that Jonathan and his armor bearer fell upon them in ambush, and such was their shock that they ran in chaos, while Jonathan slew them from the front and his armor bearer from the rear.

⁴⁸ Now when the main body of Saul's army saw the tumult arise from the enemy camp, the king called them together and they marched forth into battle. And the Philistines fell back, but the sons of Israel pursued them.

⁴⁹ When, therefore, the men of Saul's main army entered the woodlands, Jonathan rejoined them. ⁵⁰ The soldiers were in distress from hunger, for they had not eaten because of Saul's curse. For this reason, when they saw a patch of honey on the earth, not one of them stretched forth his hand. ⁵¹ But Jonathan did not shrink from it, and reached out the end of his staff, which he dipped in the honeycomb and raised to his mouth.

⁵² Then the others who were with him drew back in fear and chastened him because of his father's curse. ⁵³ But Jonathan said, "My father has caused trouble for the nation. See how my eyes brightened once I partook of this honey? ⁵⁴ How much better would it have been if all the men had eaten this day from the plunder we gained from our enemies? Would not our victory have been even greater?"

⁵⁵ But when Saul found out about this, he called all the

men together and asked Jonathan before the entire assembly, "What is it you have done," whereupon Jonathan told him.

⁵⁶ Saul then declared, "May Yahweh deal with me in the most severe manner if you do not die, Jonathan!"

⁵⁷ The people, however, rose up and said, "Should Jonathan be put to death even as he has brought deliverance to Israel? May it never be! Not a hair on his head shall fall to the ground!" ⁵⁸ And they placed themselves between Saul and Jonathan, that no harm would come to the prince.

⁵⁹ Then did Saul go forth against Moab and against Edom and against Ammon, against the kings of Zobah and all the nations round about. ⁶⁰ But there arose a schism between the king and Jonathan because the king had ordered his own son's death and the people had prevented it.

⁶¹ Then did Saul begin to fear that Jonathan should rise against him, and that the people should support him.

4

¹ Samuel saw these things and lamented all the more that he had anointed Saul over Israel. ² He therefore sought a new way to discredit him. If he would, by force of arms, establish his name as Israel's savior, perhaps then he could be undone at the sight of weakness.

³ When, therefore, Samuel learned that he planned to go

forth against the Amelekites, the Most High sought him out and, before the assembled company, delivered him this charge: "Go now forward and smite Amalek, and utterly destroy them from the face of the earth. ⁴ Spare them not, nor any of their possessions. Slay man and woman and suckling infant. Bring forth the lifeblood of ox and sheep, ass and camel."

⁵ Now Saul could not oppose this, so he went forth at the head of his army and set out toward the city of Amalek. But to the Kenites who dwelt among them, who had been allies of old to Israel, he sent word that they should depart from there, lest they be caught up in the slaughter. ⁶ Therefore did they remove themselves and flee. And the forces of Saul descended like a great storm upon Amalek. As locusts from the desert did the appear, as if from nowhere. As hail raining down from heaven, they fell with force on the city of Amalek.

⁷ The beggar on the city street, they slew him, and his cup fell to the ground with a clang as his body grew cold and lifeless.

⁸ The child playing in the road, they slew her. Her voice rose in a wail, as she fell to the ground, then cried no more.

⁹ The woman at the well, they slew her. Never seeing their approach, she died there in a single moment. Her water pail half full still. Her body empty of life.

¹⁰ The man in the field, they slew him. With the blade of his own harvester they cut him down, like a fruit tree not yet ripened. ¹¹ With his last breath, he cursed bitterly the name of their foreign god. And for his insolence, they

separated his head from his fallen body. And they said, "For the glory of our lord!"

¹¹ Ox and the ass, they slew them. Still bound to the oxcart did the oxen fall, writhing. Still tethered to the stable did the asses fall, braying.

¹² Sheep they slew, blood spattering their woolen coats.

¹³ Cattle they slew, their udders full of new white milk.

¹⁴ Women they slew in the arms of their lovers, and children they slew at the breast of their mothers.

¹⁵ The air was thick with the dying breaths of man and beast, and the streets ran red with the blood of the city's people. ¹⁴ With the edge of the sword did Saul and his minions smite all of Amalek. ¹⁵ He spared only Agag, the king of that place, from death, along with the best of the sheep and the oxen, the lambs and the fatlings. ¹⁶ Those that were healthy he preserved. The weak and the ill, he destroyed from the face of the land.

¹⁷ All these things because of Samuel's pride and murderous intentions.

¹⁸ Yet still, it was not enough to assuage the Most High. No. For the sake of what was left alive, Samuel now cursed Saul before his assembled company.

¹⁹ "Why does the bleating of sheep fill my ears? And how is it that I hear the lowing of oxen this day? ²⁰ Did not I tell you the command of Yahweh truly, to utterly destroy the wicked Amalekites? Did I not say, 'Wage war against them until you have wiped them from the face of the Earth'? ²¹ Why have you turned aside from the command of your god? Why did you do evil in his sight by taking the

plunder for yourself?"

²² Samuel then left him and, in that day, began to plot how he might overthrow him. From that moment forward, the two never again laid eyes on one another.

5

¹ Then Samuel went forth into Judah, to the town of Bethlehem, and to the House of Jesse. ² No more would he count on tiny Benjamin as his ally. Instead would he enlist strength to back his purpose.

³ Judah was the mightiest tribe in the region, and many of its proudest men held no great love of the Benjamites. ⁴ Some had felt the sting of envy when Samuel chose Saul as king from the tribe to the north of them. And even now, Jesse grew suspicious when he saw the aging priest approach his lands. ⁵ "Are you come in peace?" he asked him.

⁶ So Samuel went forth to prepare a sacrifice before him, bearing witness of his intent.

⁷ After this, the two men took counsel together. And Samuel conferred with Jesse, that they might stand against Saul's armies. ⁸ He stated his design that one of Jesse's own sons should become king of all the land, and to this proposal the old man did hearken. To it also did he gladly assent.

⁹ But Samuel in his old age was shrewd and cunning, as ever he had been. So when Jesse summoned his seven eldest sons before them, each appeared in order; yet not

one of them found favor in the eyes of Samuel. [10] He therefore said, "Is this, then, all?" For he knew that Jesse had not summoned his youngest son, and he also had it in his mind that this youngest should be the one chosen.

[11] For who save the youngest is easier to bend? Like a reed in a soft wind, he follows the voice of his teacher. [12] And who save the youngest will serve his elders more truly? Like a pup eager for a new bone, he will do his master's bidding.

[13] So it was that Jesse brought forth the youngest before him, and Samuel anointed him straightaway.

[14] And his name was David.

[15] But though the holdings of Judah were extensive and its people many, still its armies were no match for the men of Saul. [16] So it was decided that David should swear allegiance to Saul and enter into his service until an opportune moment should arise to supplant him. [17] For, as has been told, the days of Saul were bitter days of war against Philistia, and whenever Saul heard of stout-hearted men who were strong in battle, then did he take them into his own service.

[18] It was therefore arranged that one of Saul's liegemen (who in fact had pledged fealty to David) should recommend David to the king's service, saying, "He is courageous of heart and fierce in battle. His tongue is quick and his aspect is pleasing."

[19] So Saul sent word to Jesse, that he might send David to him at once, and David entered into the king's service as an armor bearer. [20] Now there are those who say that David had served in this same manner before, as armor bearer to

Jonathan. ²¹ It was this one who had declared to Jonathan, "I am with you heart and soul" when they had gone off with Saul unknowing to face the Philistines. And he had returned with him to witness the king direct his fury against Jonathan, passing against his own son a sentence of death.

²² Now, in these days, it is said that David entered into an alliance with him, and that Jonathan loved him as himself.

²³ Now why should this have been so?

²⁴ Some say it was because of the great regard that existed between them, each for the other. Yet others declare Jonathan sought to supplant Saul upon the throne. ²⁵ Others still say it was David who was plotting to seize the kingship for himself, and that Jonathan sought to preserve his own life in the event that David should succeed. ²⁶ For how should he expect to be spared should David overthrow Saul? ²⁷ For this reason, it is said, Jonathan gave David the robe of his back and his tunic, along with his bow, his sword and his belt. In so doing, he was yielding not only the symbols of his right to claim the throne, but also the signs that he should be leader of the armies.

²⁸ It was after this that the men under David's command went out in force against the nations round about them and claimed many victories, so that Saul's regard for David grew and the people acclaimed him, saying, "Saul has slain his thousands and David his ten thousands."

²⁹ From that time forward, Saul ever sought to keep

David close to him, for he did not trust him. ³⁰ He thought that by feigning goodwill toward him, he would entice the Judahite to say something that might give away his true intent, whereupon he could have him arrested and put to death. ³¹ But David was full of guile and showed no such intention, and Saul feared David's standing among the people, that they might rise up if the king slew him without cause.

³² Saul therefore said to himself, "I will offer him one of my daughters if he goes out against the Philistines in battle. ³³ I will not raise a hand against him. Let them do the dirty work for me." ³⁴ And he offered David the hand of his daughter Michal should he go forth into battle and slay a hundred Philistines.

³⁵ Yet David fulfilled his obligation and returned from the battlefield having slain even more of the enemy, so that his reputation grew. ³⁶ Saul therefore sought out another way to be rid of him, but Jonathan heard of it and warned David, saying, "My father is looking for the opportunity to kill you." ³⁷ And when Saul sent men to David's house with orders to slay him, Michal warned him and let him down through a window, so that he escaped. ³⁸ She then took an idol and placed it on the bed, covering it with a garment and crowning its head with goats' hair.

³⁹ After this, he went to Jonathan, and the two of them renewed their pact, with Jonathan saying, "Whatever it is you ask of me, this I will surely do." ⁴⁰ Yet he knew that if David should rise up against his father to claim the kingdom, the Judahite would have no further use for the

rightful heir. [41] Therefore he besought David, "Show me kindness that fails not, so long as I may live, and do not withhold your favor from my kin even after all your enemies are removed from the face of the earth."

[42] Then they renewed the pact between them, and David withdrew for fear of his life.

[43] When, therefore, David did not appear before Saul, the king grew suspicious and knew that his son had betrayed him. [44] "You son of a perverse and seditious woman! Do you not think I know that you have thrown in your lot with the son of Jesse, to your own disgrace and the shame of the woman who bore you?" (He said this because his own wife had left him and fled to David's camp.) [45] "As long as the son of Jesse shall live, neither you nor your kingdom shall be established on this earth. Therefore have him brought to me, for he must not live!"

[46] But Jonathan went forth from that place with a warning for David, who fled therefore to Gath, a city of Philistia, to the enemies of Saul and Israel. [47] There he sought to form an alliance with Achish, the ruler of that place.

[48] But Achish said, "Is this not David, the king of the land?" (He said this because David was the king of Judah, though he had sworn fealty to Saul.) [49] Achish was therefore uneasy, for he thought that David sought to trick him into lowering his guard, that Saul's forces might attack him. [50] "Is this not the man of whom they sing, 'Saul has slain his thousands, and David his ten thousands'?"

[51] David therefore, being afraid, withdrew from that

place and made an alliance with Moab, another of Israel's enemies. In this manner did he show himself a traitor, both to his king and to his country.

6

¹ From that day forward, there was great strife in the land, which was rent asunder between the men of Saul and the men of David. ² Brother took up arms against brother, and innocent blood was shed on the naked earth, all for the sake of power and greed. ³ Neither side was without blame, and the heavens turned their eyes away from the carnage.

⁴ It is said that the men made a truce between them: that David gave his oath to Saul and in his turn promised to spare the king's sons from the sword. ⁵ Yet neither man kept his word, for both men valued power over honor and wealth above integrity. ⁶ In latter days would David, when he came into the kingdom, surrender seven men from the line of Saul to the men of Gibeon to be slain. And Saul, for his part, did not long sheath his sword against his rival.

⁷ After going his way from the presence of Saul, David and his men moved south into the desert, and there did he send emissaries ahead of him to a wealthy shepherd of that region, demanding that his men be garrisoned for the night. ⁸ (It was David's custom to go roving about and require that those whom he should come across pay tribute to him, in exchange for a guarantee of peace.)

⁹ But the man refused him, saying, "Who is this David

son of Jesse that he should be as a master over me? ^{10} Many servants are casting off the snares of bondage. Why therefore should I take the bread and water, together with the meat of the animals I have slaughtered, away from my own men and give it to someone who appears out of nowhere with such demands?"

^{11} When David heard the shepherd's reply ordered his own men to strap on their swords, proclaiming, "May my god visit wrath upon me if one of the men on this shepherd's land is left alive!"

^{12} Now the shepherd was a drunkard and a glutton, for which reason he met his end before David could slay him. And David rejoiced at the shepherd's death, believing his god had answered his prayers in striking him down. Yet it was not any god who accomplished this, but the shepherd's own weak heart and thirst for spirits.

^{13} After this, David took the man's wife to be his own.

^{14} But Saul took his own daughter Michal, who had been David's wife, and gave her to another, in the same manner that a man would bestow a mare or cow upon a neighbor. Then he came against David with a force of three thousand men, but David eluded him and fled.

^{15} Once again, he sought refuge with Achish, the ruler of Gath in Philistia, forsaking his own king to whom he had pledged an oath and seeking to take up residence with his enemy. ^{16} This time, Achish received him and the six hundred men in his company, and they made a pact between them. ^{17} So did David and the kingdom of Judah withdraw their fealty from Israel and pledge an oath instead to the Philistines.

[18] David then abode in the town of Ziklag, which is between Judah and the coastal cities of Philistia, thereby sealing their compact. [19] And David served Achish faithfully, acting without mercy against the peoples of the south. [20] He led raiders against Gezer and Amalek and Geshur, all the way south toward Egypt. They were as men without heart or conscience, and wherever they went, they left not a single man or woman with breath still in their lungs. [21] In their greed, they took to themselves the sheep and asses, camels and donkeys that belonged to the people, along with even the garments of those whose blood they spilled. [22] And David cared not for the people whose lives he stole, but only that he might preserve his own, reasoning, "If I were to spare them, they might open their mouths and tell my enemies of my actions."

[23] Achish therefore placed his trust in David, so thoroughly did the King of Judah do his bidding, for he said to himself, "He has become an abomination to his own people, and such is the extent of it that he shall be bound to my service for life."

[24] Such was Achish's faith in David that, when the Philistines went forth against Saul, he wished to bring David and his men along with him. [25] "Has not this man been an officer in Saul's own army?" he said. "Yet he has been in our company more than a year now, and his record among us has been without blemish." [26] For he hoped that David would be able to provide not only men to send forth in combat, but also intelligence concerning the ways of Saul

on the battlefield.

[27] Yet the other rulers of Philistia worried that David might turn against them in the midst of the conflict and defect to Saul. Had he not already changed sides once? Could he therefore be trusted? [28] "Let David and his fighters return from whence they came, to guard the place you have assigned him," they told Achish. [29] "He must not accompany us in the field, or he will turn against us in the midst of the battle. What better way for him to regain his liege's favor than by bringing him the heads of our men?"

[30] Therefore Achish sent David away from them, but he did not turn aside and make for Saul's tents as they had feared. [31] Instead he returned to Ziklag in Philistia, for he remained in the service of Achish and his heart was steadfast against Saul.

[32] Thence did he set off again with his men to plunder the land around about, but when he returned, he found that raiders has treated him in like manner: that Ziklag had been burned to the ground and the women and children of the town had been taken captive. [33] So it was that David and his men were treated in the same fashion that they had treated others. But though they wept, they were not humbled.

[34] Instead, they pursued the raiders and overtook them, recovering all that had been taken from them while claiming the raiders' flocks and herds as their own. [35] The raiders themselves they killed, except for four hundred who fled on the backs of their camels. They scattered from that place.

³⁶ And these raiders were Amalekites.

³⁷ David's men sought to keep the plunder for themselves, but David would not allow it and instead sent the bounty to the landholders of Judah. This he meant as an inducement that they might not rise up against him.

7

¹ At this time, the Philistines pressed hard against the men of Saul and drove them back, harrying them until they scattered and fled. ² They killed Jonathan and the other sons of Saul, Abinadab and Malkishua. Their archers drew back the bowstring and launched their arrows, which found their marks.

³ One of the arrows felled Saul, and he was grievously wounded, with the enemy in pursuit. ⁴ In that hour, an Amalekite rode up and found him, and the king entreated the man, "Stand here by me and slay me, for I am at the point of death, yet still I live."

⁵ The Amalekite did as he was bidden, but he took the crown that he had worn and his armband, and he brought these things to David in Ziklag. ⁶ With him also he brought news of Saul's death, and also Jonathan's.

⁷ Now some people said to themselves, "Why was this Amalekite so far to the north of his homeland?" and also, "Why did he return with news of these things to David, unless he was in his service?" ⁸ For why should he have brought Saul's crown and armband to David, rather than to

the king's surviving son, Eshbaal? Could it not have been because David so instructed him?

⁹ For this reason it began to be whispered that David had ordered the Amalekite to go forth and slay Saul. ¹⁰ But David denied this upon receiving the report, calling down curses instead upon the Amalekite. "Your blood shall be upon your own head," he declared. "Your own mouth testifies against you in proclaiming you have slain the anointed one of Yahweh."

¹¹ He ordered his own man to kill the Amalekite, and it is said that he did so to prevent the man from testifying against him, just as he had killed all the inhabitants of the towns and countryside during the raids of the southland in former days. ¹² And publicly did he lament for Saul and for Jonathan, yet in deed did he mourn them not, but instead took the crown and set it upon his own head.

¹³ But Eshbaal became king of Israel, and the two men continued the war that had begun between David and Saul. ¹⁴ When Eshbaal sent an emissary to discuss terms for peace, the leader of David's armies, a man named Joab, slew him. But the king himself admitted no part in it and put on a show of public mourning. ¹⁵ Yet what general acts in such a way without his king's blessing? ¹⁶ Is it therefore any wonder that Joab remained in his favored post even after the king's rebuke? For lawlessness begets lawlessness, and the thirst for power is never quenched.

¹⁷ Shortly after this, Eshbaal himself was slain, and the men who did the deed brought his head to David as proof of their fealty. ¹⁸ Yet again David did not publicly condone

the act and had the two men put to death, as he had done with the Amalekite who killed Saul. [19] For David sought to portray himself as always blameless, regardless of how many men were slain as he rose to power.

[20] When, therefore, he had become strong enough, he turned against his former patrons in Philistia and rose up against them, as he had risen against Saul. [21] He turned the sword also against the Moabites, with whom he had formerly made an alliance. [22] In those days did his own men proclaim him the favorite of Yahweh, speaking to him thus on behalf of their god: "I will magnify your name, like the names of the men most esteemed in all the earth. [23] I will set aside a place for my people Israel, and will establish them so they shall dwell in a home of their own and be assailed no more. [24] No longer shall they be oppressed by wicked people, as they have been since the days in which I first appointed judges over my people. And I will give you rest from all your enemies."

[25] Yet truly, none of these promises was fulfilled, and none of these things came to pass. [26] Throughout David's reign, he was harried by his enemies. A man named Sheba rose up in rebellion against him, and his own son opposed him, and had him cast out of Jerusalem. [27] Neither did the nation he had conquered at the point of the javelin and sword find rest, for the coalition of north and south that he founded continued but a single generation.

[28] Throughout his own day he would continue to oppress his people, even those most loyal to him, should it serve his purpose to do so.

²⁹ When his son forced himself on his own daughter, then spurned her, he did not impose justice upon him nor did he remove his inheritance, but instead stood by while another of his sons brought vengeance to bear against the evildoer.

³⁰ Then he also took the inheritance of Meribbaal, the son of Jonathan (the same Jonathan to whom he had sworn many oaths) and removed it from him, giving it instead to the man who was his steward.

³¹ But perhaps the greatest of his offenses was committed against the most loyal of his followers, a Hittite named Uriah who had pledged himself to David's service. ³² In those days, David no longer went forth at the head of his armies, but instead charged his general, Joab the Slayer (for he had slain many men at David's bidding) to go forth in his stead and fight the king's battles. And Uriah went out with him, along with his fellows.

³³ But Uriah's wife remained in the city, and it came to pass that David chanced to see her bathing from the roof of his palace. She was very beautiful, and David's loins were aroused at the sight of her. ³⁴ He therefore asked as to who she was, and was told, "She is Bathsheba, the daughter of Eliam and the wife of Uriah the Hittite." ³⁵ David's lust, however, was not cooled by the fact that this woman had pledged herself to another. Nay, he desired her even so and sent messengers to bring Bathsheba to him. ³⁶ Then she went in to him (for who would dare refuse a king?), and she lay with him.

³⁷ In due course, she conceived and was with child, at

which news David was distraught. [38] He said to himself, "Surely they will know Uriah is not the father, and there are those who know that I was with her. I must summon him to return quickly, lest I be charged with a grievous act which men may use as an excuse to oppose me."

[39] He therefore sent Joab the Slayer to retrieve Uriah from the battlefield, thinking the Hittite would surely go in to his wife upon his return. [40] Yet he did not. Instead did Uriah sleep outside the entrance to the palace with all his men and retainers.

[41] When David heard of this, he summoned Uriah before him and asked him, "Why did you not return home?"

[42] But Uriah said, "My commander Joab and my lord's men are camped in the open country, sleeping in their tents. How then could I go to my house to eat and drink and lie with my wife? As I live, I could never do such a thing!"

[43] Then David tried to entice him to lie with Bathsheba by plying him with wine, yet still did Uriah lie on a mat among the servants. And he did not return home.

[44] Then David determined in the darkness of his heart that he should have Uriah slain, and this was the manner in which it should be done: [46] David sent word to Joab that he was sending Uriah back to the battlefield, where his armies had lain siege to a stronghold of the Ammonites. [47] And he told him, "Put Uriah on the front lines of the battle, where the fighting is heaviest, and then pull back without alerting him, that he might be struck down and perish on the field."

[48] Joab therefore did as his king had commanded, and Uriah was left alone in the field to be slain by the enemy. [49] But David did not mourn for him. Instead, he took Bathsheba to himself for his wife, so that the child should not be thought a bastard and he himself should not be accused.

[50] Even so was a charge brought against him, but no punishment did he endure. Instead, it was judged that the child he had fathered with Bathsheba should die. [51] So it was that David's dishonor was visited instead upon an innocent babe, and the blood on David's own hands was multiplied by the child's death. [52] The blame for this was cast at the feet of Yahweh, yet would any god's judgment slay an innocent babe for the folly of a king?

[52] Indeed, a king has the greatest of power, and can bring something to pass most easily without the need for any guile. [53] Yet a babe has no potency of his own, neither shame nor guilt, and is reliant in the whole on others to care for and minister to him. [54] How, therefore, is it just that the most vulnerable should be punished for the trespass of the most potent?

[55] These questions were not for David to answer, nor for his heir or those who came after them. As generations fell and new generations rose in their stead, men made wars against one another without ceasing. [56] The kingdom David had built was rent asunder once more, as it had been in the days of war between Saul and the son of Jesse. [57] Kings rose and fell, and their realms fell after them, swallowed by the armies of Nebuchadnezzar and Cyrus, Xerxes and

Alexander. [58] Thereafter were they lost to the mists of time or magnified in the cause of new kings who pillaged the false glory of their fathers. [59] Old gods were reviled in the name of new gods, and newer gods still were given homage.

[60] So it is that the world is turned on its head when men presume to speak for the gods, placing words in their mouths that are neither true nor honorable. [61] Over these words do men make war with one another, shedding the blood of their kinsmen for the sake of falsehoods and petty jealousies, over the lusts of kings and the writings of priests long dead. [62] These words they enshrine on stone tablets and sacred scrolls locked away in vaults of gold and silver.

[63] They speak "peace, peace," yet they set upon one another like ravening wolves, for the sake of pride and power.

[65] They preserve not acts of love or marvels of skill and artistry, but instead the sagas of wars so common they seem ceaseless and fill ream upon ream of their chronicles. [66] Let these stories be a lesson to those that read them, not a lesson to be emulated, but to be abhorred. Not those in which to take glory, but in which to take shame.

[67] For the world was not fashioned by a creator in blood and tears and broken dreams. Neither was it built on sorrow and regret. [68] But it is fashioned by the hands of those whose honor exceeds their bloodthirst, and whose integrity surpasses false piety. [69] As it is fashioned, so is it also preserved as long as women of honor and men of virtue sustain it.

[70] This is the testament of Osiris, that each one should fight his own battles without visiting them upon his neighbor. That learning should always precede declaration. That kindness should swallow bitterness. That dignity should stand foursquare in the path of oppression.

[71] Neither look back at the age of the gods in longing nor wish for their return, for to humble one's self and honor one's fellow is the beginning of godhood. Its end lies not in power, but understanding.

Stephen H. Provost

The author writes about American highways, mutant superheroes, mythic archetypes and pretty much anything he wants. A journalist, historian, philosopher and novelist, he lives on the Central Coast of California. And he loves cats. Read his blogs and keep up with his latest activities at stephenhprovost.com.

www.ingramcontent.com/pod-product-compliance
Lightning Source LLC
LaVergne TN
LVHW051506080426
835509LV00017B/1950